Secrets of a Successful Employee Recognition System

DANIEL C. BOYLE

Secrets of a Successful Employee Recognition System

PUBLISHER'S MESSAGE BY NORMAN BODEK

PRODUCTIVITY PRESS
PORTLAND, OREGON

Productivity Press
P.O. Box 13390
Portland, OR 97213-0390
United States of America
Telephone: 503-235-0600
Telefax: 503-235-0909

ISBN: 1-56327-083-8

Cover design by Leigh Wells
Book and text design by William Stanton
Composition and graphics by Teutschel Design Services, Palo Alto, CA
Printed and bound by Maple-Vail in the United States of America

Library of Congress Cataloging-in-Publication Data:

Boyle, Daniel C.
    Secrets of a successful employee recognition system / Daniel C. Boyle
        p.   cm.
    Includes bibliographical references.
    ISBN 1-56327-083-8
    1. Incentives in industry. 2. Incentive awards. 3. Suggestion systems.   I. Title
HF5549.5.I5B69   1995
658.3'142—dc20   94 - 47661
                                                                                         CIP

99 98 97 96 95   10 9 8 7 6 5 4 3 2 1

This work is dedicated to

every person who ever yearned

to be the recipient of the words

"Thanks for doing a good job!"

and to every person who ever said

"Thank you" and meant it.

Contents

Publisher's Message

Productivity Press has led the industry in offering our readers nuts-and-bolts details on how to establish employee involvement, empowered teams, and continuous improvement methods in the workplace. The essence of all of these is what Ryuji Fukuda, our very first author, calls a "no-blame environment."

How does a manager establish "no blame" on the shop floor or in an office while driving quality, cost, and delivery standards to optimal levels? Dan Boyle says you do it by saying "Thank you" to your steady employees for their continual effort, for being on time, for showing up, for doing the jobs they are paid to do without complaint day after day. This book is not about incentive systems. It's about recognition of unsung heroes who slog it out week after week, year after year. It really is about the power of saying "Thank you"!

Now, that may seem too simple an idea, but think about what goes on in most business environments. "Thank you" may not be something you hear very often from managers or supervisors. What has gone wrong, or is about to, is what captures everyone's focus most of the time. Who did it is always the next question. What went wrong and who did it.

Some companies have shifted to what went wrong and *what* did it — a process focus. This is a quantum leap toward no blame. But it's still very hard to keep a process focus when what went wrong is the only issue ever addressed by a manager. You usually get down to the who sooner or later. What is needed for a process focus to take hold is an environment of trust and appreciation. Then when the *who* issue arises during problem solving, people responsible for the process under scrutiny will feel safe enough to consider new ways of doing things. They know they are appreciated for the effort they make every day to do their jobs well. They want to find ways to do it better — and they are glad to be asked. A "shoot the messenger" mentality no longer exists and they know it — and that makes the difference.

Saying "Thank you," Boyle observes, leads to improvement suggestions. And without having to focus on those who are not coming every day or may be shirking while they are there, peer pressure begins to bring those people around too. Time and again, Boyle has seen his approach raise the slackers to the level of the sloggers and turn the sloggers into inspired and creative problem solvers.

In *Secrets of a Successful Employee Recognition System,* Boyle shows that focusing on what goes right and who did it is the first step toward initiating employee involvement and establishing cost-saving suggestion systems. Chapter 1 tells the engaging story of how he came up with his 100 Club Solution, as he calls it, to reach a disenchanted workforce at a unionized paper products plant. In Chapter 2, Boyle describes, step by step, how to set up a 100 Club in any type of organization. Chapter 3 is filled with detailed examples of implementations in organizations ranging from industrial plants to professional offices, nonprofits, small businesses, and even educational institutions. Additional materials compare 100 Club results with U.S. and Japanese suggestion system statistics, present a third-party report on the 100 Club implementation at Diamond International, define key terms, and list further reading describing the 100 Club or implementations at particular sites.

Dan Boyle has helped implement this simple 100 Club approach in hundreds of organizations across America, in Europe, and in South Africa. And everywhere he goes he leaves smiling workers behind him. Smiling workers mean that you are on the path to empowerment, to vital suggestion systems, to continuous improvement that adds up to significant cost savings companywide.

Sound too good to be true? Read this great little book and find out how your business can hum with the sound of "Thank you."

We want to thank Dan Boyle for choosing to publish with us. Thanks also to the editorial team: Julie Zinkus, Mary Junewick, Vivina Ree, Janis LaRue, Martha Wagner, and Karen Jones; to the production team: William Stanton and Susan Swanson; and to Teutschel Design Services, graphics and page composition.

Norman Bodek
Publisher

Diane Asay
Editor-in-chief

Acknowledgments

Completion of this work would not have been possible without the encouragement and support of some very special people.

I am grateful to my mother, Margaret Mary (Donahue) Boyle and my late father, John, for instilling in me — through their example — the importance of recognizing people for their good efforts.

I am indebted to Andrew Rock, who started out as my agent and ended up a dear friend. He constantly reminded me that patience is a virtue — especially when it comes to what seemed to be a never-ending search for the right publisher.

At Productivity Press, I am deeply appreciative for the efforts of my editor, Diane Asay, and her assistant, Mary Junewick, and to Beth Simone and Carla Comarella for *their* patience with me.

Mostly, I am thankful to my wife and best friend, Angela, without whose encouragement and gentle prodding I never would have completed this book. This odyssey is exciting because of you!

Introduction

For seven and a half years, Mary Ann Roberts worked in the quality control department at Marcus Printing Company in Holyoke, Massachusetts. For almost the same length of time, she kept to herself an idea she thought would streamline specific aspects of her company's quality-control process and save the business some money.

One afternoon, Mary Ann Roberts got up from her desk and dropped a 14-word note into the company's suggestion box. Mary Ann Roberts' suggestion now nets Marcus Printing about $18,000 a year.

What took Mary Ann Roberts seven and a half years to speak up?

"I wanted to be the first employee at Marcus Printing to get a 100 Club jacket," explained Mary Ann. "After looking at the different ways to score 100 points, I realized the best way I could beat out everybody else was to make suggestions. And I had a terrific suggestion."

What finally motivated Mary Ann Roberts to make her suggestion was the newly implemented 100 Club Employee Recognition System, which was designed by Marcus Printing's management and employees to recognize the ordinary day-to-day contributions each employee makes to the success of the printing business.

"And this is no word of a lie," Mary Ann Roberts continued, adjusting her silver-framed glasses. "I wanted to help the company, which was going through some pretty tough times. I thought my suggestion would help me keep a good job."

Today, few workers in the United States or elsewhere have the opportunity to gain instant recognition for doing a good job — for doing the kind of work their employers routinely expect them to do. In my view, personal and immediate recognition is an employee's inalienable right. It is the key that drives an employee beyond his or her own expectations, to maintain high performance levels, to fill a deeply felt need, to be part of a finely tuned team.

Immediate praise and recognition from our supervisors, or even from our co-workers, puts us in touch with life's energy in a far more fulfilling way than does a paycheck. But today, percentages and ratios and other abstractions make the measure of our daily efforts more arcane. Perhaps in a preindustrial workplace the measure of one's daily efforts was more obvious to one's co-workers, families, and anyone else who cared to look. Who knows? But in today's workplace, personal and immediate recognition for doing what is expected is rare.

WHAT'S IN THIS BOOK

This small book contains all the information any manager needs to install a 100 Club Employee Recognition System.

Chapter 1 describes a little bit about my background and how the 100 Club Employee Recognition System came to be. It should take you about 10 minutes to read. This background material will be helpful when you read Chapter 2.

Chapter 2 explains how to design a 100 Club Employee Recognition System for any organization, including yours. It should take you about 18 minutes to read.

Chapter 3 contains examples that show how various organizations, large and small, successfully installed the 100 Club Employee Recognition System. This is fascinating stuff. You can whiz through it, or spend longer, as I do, marveling at the way each management and employee team designs its very own 100 Club Employee Recognition System.

I used to hesitate to talk too much about the 100 Club Employee Recognition System. I'm not sure why. Maybe because it seems so corny, so obvious, so hokey in a down-to-earth, neighborly sort of way. Maybe it's because I'm just a news reporter who fell into the business world with fresh eyes and dumb luck. I don't have an MBA or any unusual academic credentials.

Maybe I always hesitate to talk about the 100 Club Employee Recognition System because I already made my money from the idea: It helped me buy and sell that multimillion-dollar Palmer plant for which I worked. Perhaps, now, however, like Mary Ann Roberts of Marcus Printing (one of my favorite people in this world), I am motivated to talk about the 100 Club Employee Recognition System — that is, to drop this small book into the national suggestion box — because I want to be the first on my block to get a 100 Club jacket.

I want to thank you for reading this introduction. I encourage you to continue to read on for just a few more minutes and just a few more pages. I guarantee you are about to learn something that will improve your organization's performance and add profits to your organization's bottom line.

1

Discovering the Language of Points

Among American workers, I have been lucky. At 18, I started working at a waxed paper manufacturing operation in Holyoke, Massachusetts. The company's owner, Larry Graham, was an excellent role model. His manner was exemplar of all that I find best in organization management. Among other things, he was interested in those with whom he worked. He spent much of his time on the production floor, supervising, training, and talking with his employees. At the end of the workday, when I passed his desk coming around from the time clock, he'd never fail to wave and say, "Hey, thanks, Danny. See you tomorrow."

I got a tremendous break when I landed my second job as a general-assignment reporter for a daily newspaper, the Holyoke *Transcript-Telegram*. This was lucky for two reasons: I was paid for doing work I loved and whenever I did a good job I got a byline over my work product. People who read the newspaper often commented on what a good job I did. Recognition was my daily bread, and I couldn't get enough of it. Time and again, recognition drove me to get the story, to get it right, and to get it before reporters from other papers got it. What a great environment for a young kid to learn about life and work!

After 11 years in the work force I was offered a new job as personnel manager at a plant in Palmer, Massachusetts, just north of Holyoke. Before accepting, I visited my father at his place of work.

He worked in the shipping department of the Acme Chain Manufacturing Company in Holyoke. He punched a time clock, turning down promotions to management positions because he said he felt more secure as an hourly employee.

My father was a quiet, soft-spoken man whose family meant more to him than anything in life and whose commitment to his employer ranked a close second. One of six children, my father was born and raised in Lincoln, New Hampshire, once a small paper mill town, now a booming tourist haven. He met my mother, Margaret Mary Donahue, when she moved to Lincoln to teach high school. Growing up in their home, I was never at a loss for nurturing, recognition, security, or clearly defined responsibilities. And, so, on the day I went to talk to my father about my new job offer, I was enthusiastic and could hardly contain my glee as I enumerated to him the responsibilities I would be assigned. I was surprised by how much my father seemed to know about my future employer, and the plant's problems. He spoke about how important the plant has been to Palmer and other neighboring communities up and down the Connecticut River Valley.

"It's Palmer's second largest employer, Dad. The annual payroll is more than seven million."

"It's a thankless place to labor," my father said with uncharacteristic directness. "I'm glad you got the job, Danny. They need someone smart like you. And I mean that. The Palmer plant has a lousy reputation. Being personnel manager at the Palmer plant will be a bit like being the guy who washes the circus elephants. Big job."

THE PALMER PLANT

When I look back on it now, it seems life had blessed me with everything I needed to succeed as the personnel manager of the Palmer plant. I was determined to make a difference for the employees. I wanted them to know their efforts — individually and collectively — were appreciated. I wanted them to understand they would be recognized not only for their occasional mistakes, but for their overall good performance. I believed I would fail if employees felt, as my father did, that while doing a good job to the best of his ability he just blended into the rank and file and received management's attention only when he made a mistake.

In 1934, the world's first molded-pulp egg carton was manufactured on the north side of Palmer, Massachusetts, in a typical red brick, New England smokestack monument to nineteenth century American industrial architecture. They say the building was modern once, but as I walked through the main gate on my first day as the new personnel manager for Diamond International Corporation's Palmer plant, I had the feeling the walls and stair treads in that building were as old as anything Europe had to offer.

The smell, the sounds, the gray-chilled air, the sun piercing through the postage-stamp window lights 30 feet above the floor, made me think of all the daughters and sons of immigrants who must have labored under that roof.

Each day, through the main gate on their way to manufacture molded-pulp egg cartons marched 341 employees, most of whom were represented by United Paperworkers International Union, Local 1847. Every day the operation produced 1,600,000 egg cartons. That means 19,200,000 eggs had to be laid every day just to fill the cartons manufactured at the Palmer plant in one 24-hour cycle.

Though my office was reasonably isolated, the production area reverberated with intense noise, while hundreds of people doing the fast walk moved back and forth toward unknown and unseen destinations. All the while, bells and lights and sirens screamed for attention from someone who evidently had stepped out to the bathroom.

For decades, Diamond competed against Packaging Corporation of America for dominance in the ever-growing egg carton market. But by the 1980s, both companies were losing an uphill battle against a new, less labor-intensive product line of Styrofoam egg cartons manufactured by chemical firms such as Dalco and Mobil. Labor was viewed as a root problem at Diamond.

All egg cartons produced in the Palmer plant were made from recycled paper, including newspapers, over-issue newspaper, trim from telephone books, and some cardboard. At the north end of the plant, following one of a dozen formulas, paper was dumped into a pulper and mixed with chemicals and extremely hot water. Pulped and beaten until it turned into a slurry, it was transferred through a piping system to what was referred to as the "wet end" of the machine.

Once on the wet end, the slurry was sucked into egg carton forms by vacuum and passed through an oven heated to more than 600 degrees. After the oven, a reverse vacuum forced the cartons out of the dry forms and onto conveyor belts that carried them through a dry-press operation, which finished the cartons to a more smooth condition. The cartons went through a printing process that added a customer's name, address, UPC code, etc. Finally, they were wrapped in bundles of 250 and transferred out the south end of the plant to the warehouse for shipment.

In one variation of this totally automated manufacturing process, unprinted egg cartons had to be lifted manually off the conveyor belts when the printer setup people were changing printing plates. These unprinted cartons were referred to as "in-process cartons." Later, when the printer resumed operation, several employees, including the printer operator and the dry-press operator, were responsible for hand-feeding the in-process cartons back onto the conveyor belts. Only through the addition of these in-process cartons could higher machine productivity be achieved at the Palmer plant.

GETTING TO KNOW EACH OTHER

"You must be the new personnel guy," someone said to me in the hall. He had on a white T-shirt and blue jeans. Bright red ink covered his hands, wrists, and forearms.

After I introduced myself, a younger pressman dressed quite the same said, "I'm surprised Arnold hired a new personnel manager. We thought he'd rather close this place like he did at the Middletown plant."

"As far as I know, Bob Arnold isn't planning to close anything down. In fact, he's asked me to work on improving the relationship between management and employees. That doesn't sound like a guy who's ready to quit," I laughed. "Besides, he needs a job, too."

"So, what kind of guy are you, Boyle?" The older man was more aggressive.

"I've had a lot of jobs," I said. "Do you know Ray Beaudry?" They both nodded enthusiastically.

"Ray Beaudry helped me become the first non-cardcarrying-union person named to the Eagle Lodge of Papermakers' Committee for Political Action." I let that earful sink in for a minute. "We've been friends for over 25 years. If you have more questions about what kind of guy I am, I suggest you call Ray."

On the way back to my office, I couldn't help but wonder if my boss, Bob Arnold, the plant manager, had deliberately misled me about his commitment to improve the relationship between management and employees. It was obvious, even on my first day, that morale among the employees was snake-belly high. By the end of the week, I was picking up real hostility.

As personnel manager, my responsibilities included every imaginable aspect of human resources from the day a person completes a job application to the day the employee is fired, quits, retires, or dies.

I coordinated the pension plan with our experts in the Manhattan corporate offices; served as a sounding board when employees had new ideas; was referee when a dispute arose among employees or between supervisors and their workers. I was to try to resolve contract issues before a grievance was filed. I was the chief negotiator at contract time. I was to listen intently when employees, regardless of rank or position, tried to wrestle with work or personal problems. And I had to remain firm when an employee was being terminated.

It didn't take long for me to get a feeling for how much time our department managers were spending on employees whose work habits negatively affected production. This reality was driven home in my second month, when I attended a fourth-step grievance meeting one hot and humid Friday afternoon.

Grievance actions between management and union employees follow a strict protocol. What can't be resolved at a first-step grievance meeting, goes to a second, etc. A fourth-step grievance meeting addresses the most serious and difficult issues. At a fourth-step grievance meeting the company is represented by the plant manager and the local union by its international representative. At Diamond, this meant Bob Arnold squared off against affable veteran labor organizer Walter Riley. Riley was a character, who deliberately misspoke to convey a country-boy innocence. Physically, he resembled Archie Bunker, a characterization enhanced by his abuse of the English language.

On this one June afternoon, Riley was particularly dismayed by the 14 different issues on the agenda. Of the 14 matters, only 3 could truly be described as alleged violations of the union contract. The other 11 matters were more pet peeves that made their way through the grievance process only because of the strictly adversarial relationship existing between management and labor.

Three hours of grumbling and griping had produced some agreement, but with at least two issues headed toward arbitration, Riley commented, "I can't keep coming back here week after week to resolve the same old problems. Why can't you folks just try to work things out? Wouldn't this plant be better served if you spent more time making egg cartons?"

"Riley," said Bob Arnold, "I couldn't agree with you more."

"Well, I don't know how to run a big old plant like this, but if I did I wouldn't give a squat if them boys at the shipping dock played their radios, as long as they got the work done. And I sure as hell wouldn't spend a beautiful afternoon like this trying to convince a narrow-minded fat ass like me that they shouldn't play them radios."

Walking back to the office with Bob Arnold was a quiet journey. "Listen, Bob," I said, "I have an idea I've been working on. It's a little bit off the wall, but I think it might help reduce these four-hour marathons with Riley."

Arnold smiled the smile of an exhausted man. "Do it, Dan," he said and closed the door to his office a bit harder than I think he intended.

RESEARCHING AN IDEA

Although there were a lot of indicators, I felt I needed to quantify my perception of the high level of alienation that existed between management and employees. So, I did what comes naturally to personnel managers: I conducted an informal survey.

The questions were:

1. Would you like to see a plant newspaper?

2. How do you like the food offered in the canteen?

3. Does management treat you with respect?

4. Do you approach your work with an optimistic or a pessimistic attitude?

5. Do you feel you're rewarded for a job well done?

The results were:

1. Not only did 100% of employees want a plant newspaper, many volunteered to write articles, draw cartoons, and help with the layout.

2. 63% did not like the food at the canteen.

3. 65% said they felt they were not treated respectfully by management.

4. 56% said they approached their work with a pessimistic attitude.

5. 79% said they felt they were not rewarded for a job well done.

Armed with the combination of my survey results and the memory of the grievance meeting experience, I began to draft my plan to change things. Being an Irish Catholic from a working class background, I came up with what is, I guess, a pretty structured approach.

My objectives were three:

1. To open up communications between management and employees.

2. To spend as much time praising employees as chastising them.

3. To instill the feeling that both management and employees had common objectives (i.e., keeping our jobs).

Saying "Thank you" and "You're welcome" is bedrock communication. It's my experience, if someone says "Thank you" often enough, it's pretty hard not to say "You're welcome." So, I concluded, if we said "Thank you" often enough, we would open up communication between management and employees and the first objective would be satisfied.

If the objective were to say "Thank you" as often as possible, it seemed we should design a way of saying "Thank you" to employees who did, day-in, day-out, what they were supposed to do: "Thank you for coming to work." "Thank you for not being late." "Thank you for not deliberately mucking up the in-process carton printing on press #3."

Saying "Thank you" to someone for doing what they are supposed to do is a legitimate form of praise. So, I calculated, if we said "Thank you" every day, we absolutely would be praising our employees as much as chastising them, and we would thereby satisfy the second objective.

Satisfying the third and final objective was easy. All we had to do was let our employees know that if they did what they were supposed to do, nothing more or less, we — management and employees together — would achieve our common goal: keeping our jobs.

(Actually, I wasn't convinced we could guarantee our jobs simply by getting everyone to do what they were supposed to do, but it was a cogent argument and presented both management and employees with a common objective.)

The work habits I selected for which we would say "Thank you" were attendance, punctuality, and on-the-job safety. These were normal management expectations over which each employee had total and individual control. Conformance could be objectively measured. Increased attention to attendance, punctuality, and on-the-job safety would yield increased productivity. Also, data on those work habits were already being generated.

How to say "Thank you" had to be mechanical. It had to be devoid of favoritism and it had to be positive. "Thank you for not having an accident. Here is something for you." "Thank you for coming to work and being on time. Here is something for you."

Determining what to give our employees for doing what they were supposed to do was a knotty problem. Finally, I settled on a system of giving "points" to employees. They would automatically get points every month, unless they were absent, late, or had an accident. When they accumulated 100 points they would receive a low-cost symbolic token of appreciation from top management. It all seemed logical to me. I named the program the "100 Club."

When I ran the basics of the 100 Club by Bob Arnold, he looked at me over the top of his glasses for a long time. Finally, he smiled. "What the hell," he said. "Let's run it by New York."

New York meant the vice president of Manufacturing at corporate headquarters, George Trapezoid. "I don't believe in financial incentive programs, Mr. Boyle. Besides, let me give you a little background. The Palmer plant has been losing so much money for the last three years we'd be better off shutting the place down tomorrow. Among the four plants in your division, Palmer is in third place and sinking fast in both product and profit. That is a miserable picture for me to have to look at every morning. The fact is, the entire division has to improve or face plant closings."

Before we broke for lunch, Trapezoid turned to Bob Arnold. "Prepare a cost evaluation for the Boyle idea."

"We'll do it this weekend, right, Dan?"

"Right, Bob," I said. Talk about having one's butt on the line!

I reviewed the Palmer plant performance in the areas of attendance, punctuality, and safety for the last three years. That weekend, Bob Arnold and I determined that an improvement of just 10 percent in each category would net a first-year savings of between $14,000 and $15,000. We decided the low-cost token of management's appreciation would be a lightweight nylon jacket embroidered with the company's name. If all 341 employees reached 100 points in one year, the maximum cash outlay would be $7,000.

Over the speaker phone in Bob Arnold's office, I heard George Trapezoid say, "Your plant's performance is so bad, Arnold, I don't think it can hurt."

IRONING OUT THE KINKS

During the early development of the Palmer plant 100 Club, what began as a way to focus attention on attendance, punctuality, and safety grew to include several other traits of individual employee performance. In addition, upon discussing the 100 Club concept with department managers, each manager seemed to have a compelling reason for rewarding department-specific performance traits.

In Maintenance, employees typically tended to pit craft against craft instead of working together to solve a problem. For example, when a machine broke down, a millwright might go to the scene long enough to say, "This isn't my job. You better call an electrician." Or, a machine-repair person might counter, "This isn't my job; call a millwright." In hopes of fostering teamwork within his department, the plant engineer suggested the 100 Club award points not only for individual effort, but for departmentwide efforts, too. For example, if unscheduled machine downtime reached a particular goal, everybody in the department would get some points.

In Shipping, the warehouse manager wanted to show appreciation to those workers who helped him stay within the budgeted hours of overtime each month. So, he asked that points be awarded to all employees in his department when their overtime budgets were met.

In Production, the manager wanted to reach his production targets. But, he didn't want product quality to suffer as employees worked to attain their goals. So, he asked that points be awarded to all employees assigned to specific machines when their machine reached shiftwide goals. If quality mistakes were made, the points would not be awarded, and employees would face disciplinary action, as usual.

In Accounting, the manager wanted to be sure employees were completing assignments on time and taking advantage of vendor discounts. So, he suggested points be awarded on a monthly basis as these goals were met.

In Customer Service and Sales, timeliness and accuracy of billing were the key objectives, as were getting sales representatives to meet specific sales objectives and to provide timely itineraries and expense reports. So, points were awarded as employees attained these goals.

In every case representatives of management and volunteer employees from within each department worked together to decide on the goals. The goals were based on work habits managers had always expected of their employees, and about which employees had always been aware.

The biggest disagreement occurred when we discussed how we could thank employees for coming up with "cost-saving ideas." Production workers participating in these discussions complained that maintenance people would have a better chance to score points for cost-saving ideas than any other group of employees. "They work with the engineers and are the most knowledgeable about the intricacies of the systems and processes," they reasoned.

About this time, I realized just how much people were buying into the concept of the 100 Club. I was starting to have fun. At the same time, I was worried about making the 100 Club too complicated. If it got too complicated, it would fail.

In resolving this issue, I tried to keep focused on the company's primary advantage for establishing "employee cost-saving suggestions" as a point category. It wasn't the "cost-saving" that was so important, it was the communication between employees and management.

This being the case, I played Solomon: "Let's just award one point to anyone who makes any suggestion about anything, even if it doesn't directly save money." Suddenly everybody at the table was all ears. "And, if and when the idea is implemented, the employee will receive two points."

"Do you mean I can get a point for making a suggestion about anything?" someone said.

"Well," I responded, my mind racing to keep up with the

implications of what I was recommending, "if your suggestion is for Bob Arnold to suck eggs, you're not going to get a point. But, if you make an honest, sincere suggestion, even if it doesn't work, yes, I think you should get a point."

Suddenly the meeting room was as animated as any Disney cartoon I've seen.

The union president visited me in my office. "I would like to know what's going on. Certain members of my union are secretly meeting with management. They say you are involved, too. Before I take any official action, I thought you would like to tell me your side of the story."

I asked him to keep what I was going to tell him about the 100 Club to himself and began to explain. Finally he said, "It's an incentive program."

"No, it is not an incentive program. It is an employee recognition system. And there are major differences between the two."

He sat down. I explained: "The 100 Club intends to recognize employees for good work habits, those things our managers have always expected from them. When an employee continues to display those good habits. the recognition we give takes the form of 'points.' When 100 points are accumulated, the employee receives a fleece-lined nylon jacket with the company's logo and the words, 'The 100 Club' silk-screened over the heart."

"That's it?" the union president asked.

"No. At 50-point intervals, from 150 to 600 points, there are a variety of nominally priced gifts from which employees can choose. The value of the gifts at the 150-point level is about $15.00. At the 600-point level, the value of the gifts is about $130.00. For the average employee, I figure, it will take about four years to get to the 600-point plateau."

"That's it?"

"No." I said. "From my experience, financial incentive programs are geared to get employees to perform tasks at levels never-before achieved. When these goals are met the reward is a cash prize, a vacation, a high-priced item such as a TV or a VCR. Productivity is affected by financial incentives. It goes up and down, up and down.

"The 100 Club is not designed to increase profits. It is designed to say "Thank you" to your union members for doing what is expected of them. The company hopes the 100 Club will generate goodwill from all employees. I believe that goodwill will affect productivity, which hopefully will affect everybody's job security."

"Well," the union president said getting up from his chair, "I hope everything works out with your 100 Club."

"I hope you'll be a big part of the action," I said. "Thank you for your interest."

"You're welcome," he answered.

LAUNCHING THE 100 CLUB

We had done a pretty good job of keeping the particulars of the 100 Club a secret from the rank and file, so when it came time to launch the system, there was a lot of interest.

"We've taken you for granted for as long as you've worked for us and we don't intend to do that any more."

When plant manager Bob Arnold formally launched the 100 Club by saying those words to employees gathered before the start of each shift, little did we foresee the volume of stored-up emotions that were about to be unleashed.

"For as long as this plant has been here, the only employees receiving attention were those whose work habits had a negative impact on our business," admitted the plant manager. "The attention grabbers have been those who get disciplined for things like absenteeism, tardiness, poor quality, inattention to duty, and so forth. The 100 Club is intended to change this tradition. It will reward those of you who do a good job. After all, that's the way it should be!"

Bob briefly described the mechanics of the 100 Club and we had printed handouts that gave more details. "Are there any questions?" Bob asked. "Comments?"

Joe Maloney, the first-shift mechanic known for his obstinate behavior piped up. "Forget about the jacket and those other things. Just give me 50 bucks more in my paycheck."

"The value of the gifts is nominal, Joe. We all know that," I responded. "The reason for the 100 Club is to say "Thank you" for the normally good job you do — day-in and day-out."

When Maloney didn't have a comeback I looked to his left and my eyes locked with those of Stella Antowicz, a machine operator in her late forties who had worked at Diamond for 20 years or more. She'd been a union steward more than once.

"We've had the union in this plant since 1963 and ever since, anything we've ever gotten outta the company has come from hard-fought negotiations. Now, you want us to believe that out of the goodness of your heart, you're going to start giving us a jacket and gifts for doing the same thing we've always done here?" She was shaking as she spoke. Her face was contorted in a sneer.

"You've done a good job of grasping the essence of the 100 Club, Stella."

"Excuse me, Mr. Hotshot, if I don't believe you!"

A young man who was training as a production worker on the

first shift said, "I don't think people believe this is for real. I mean, what can you do to prove it to them? To me, too?"

"Time is the best teacher, José." I said. "Let's just give the 100 Club a chance and see what happens."

A few weeks after the 100 Club got underway, the local union president stopped me as I made my rounds on the production floor. He seemed a little sheepish and almost whispered when he said, "I'd like to talk with you. Today, if possible."

We set the time and he came to my office. I closed the door and he seemed to relax as we made small talk, then: "Off the record, Dan. This 100 Club isn't going to fly unless we do something about it. Nobody wants to get out in front of it. I'm having a hard time getting people to take it seriously."

"What are they saying?"

"They think that hidden somewhere under all the bullshit there's a trick. Some strings are attached to make them work harder for the same amount of money." He paused. "I've talked to Riley about it. He thinks, as I do, that you're a square shooter. But I got to tell you, this union isn't going to drag its members into the tunnel of love."

"So, what do you think?" I said.

"Riley thinks you should speak to the membership, away from the plant — maybe at a union meeting."

"What do you think?"

"Actually, it was my idea," he said.

"Then I'll do it. How soon? What can I do to get most of your members to attend? Let me know."

"I will. Thanks, Dan."

"You're very welcome, Pete."

CONVINCING THE UNION

Local 1847, United Paperworkers, held their monthly meetings at the Knights of Columbus Hall off Route 32 in Ware, Massachusetts, a rural blue-collar community of fewer than 7,000 residents. I'd always felt at home in Ware. Boys with black motorcycle jackets and engineer boots used to scare the hell out of me when I was thirteen or fourteen, until one day in Ware at a gas station I learned by talking to boys dressed in that uniform just how regular they were.

I had never been to this Knights of Columbus Hall. It was about a 10-minute drive from the plant. I hoped there would be a large turnout, but I wasn't confident. I heard no scuttlebutt about it at the plant. The day had been unusually warm, 73 degrees. Spring was in the air. I figured the members would have better things to do on such a terrific night.

Just as that last thought formed in my mind, I realized I might be wrong. I hadn't reached the K of C, but cars, pickup trucks, and vans lined both sides of the road as I approached. I finally managed to squeeze my car into a space about 75 yards from the building.

Walking into the hall, I exchanged greetings with a number of employees. About 200 people were there. Thankfully, the windows were open and the spring-like night breeze freshened the air.

Although I'd worked at Diamond for almost a year, and knew most of the employees by name, it was hard to recognize many of the faces because of how jammed together we all were. But, I knew Joe Maloney was there when I heard him yell, "Never mind the 'hellos.' Just get down to business and tell us about the hidden strings." Maloney's challenge generated a widespread murmur of agreement.

Out of nowhere, Pete, the union president, appeared. He took my elbow and led me to the end of the bar to a raised platform. The room got so quiet I could hear the beer cooler generators humming.

I thanked them for inviting me and told them there were strings tied to the 100 Club, but they weren't hidden. "In order for you to get points for attendance, you have to come to work. You can't miss any time. But, that's the same string that has always been attached to your job with our company.

"In order for you to get points for punctuality, you have to come into work on time and work your entire shift. Again, that's the same string that's always been attached to your continuing employment.

"If you want to get points for safety, you have to go without a lost-time industrial accident. But that string has always been attached to your job with our company. That string will also help you keep your limbs and digits intact so you can enjoy your retirement."

I was astonished at how quiet the room remained. All those faces looking up to me, not talking, not drinking, not nudging. Earnestness and the desire to believe filled those faces. Even today it chokes me up to think how much those 200 people wanted to hear something, maybe anything that validated their worth in the eyes of the company for which they had worked for so long.

"In the area of productivity, in order for you to score points, you must hit the productivity targets set by each of your departments. But, this string has always been attached — not only to your employment, but to whether our plant can continue to compete in the marketplace. All of our jobs rely on improved productivity — Bob Arnold's job, my job, and your jobs — they all rely on improved productivity.

"Aside from what I just described, there are no strings attached to the 100 Club. If you still think there are, then you have created them in your own minds.

"The 100 Club is an employee recognition system that's long overdue at the Palmer plant. You heard Bob Arnold. We've taken you and your good work habits for granted for too long. We are trying to change that. All we need is a chance."

SEEING THE FIRST RESULTS

As the end of the 100 Club's first month neared, it was time to start tallying the points employees were scoring. As I checked the reports each day, I knew employees were scoring points, but I hadn't developed a recording procedure.

Keeping track of the points for 341 employees and eight departments might have been a more formidable task if the activities being monitored were not already being tracked. All the necessary raw data were in binders stacked on the floor of my office. It was a matter of organizing it and not going crazy in the meantime. "Time to wash the elephants," I said to myself.

I asked Bob Arnold for a part-time person to help track the points. Unfortunately, that expense had not been included in the cost evaluation we sent to George Trapezoid. My phone rang one morning. Mr. Arnold and Mr. Trapezoid wanted me to join them at 11:30.

"Based on the productivity increases we are tracking for this month, I think it's important to let the employees know how many points they are scoring. I'd like to hire a part-time record keeper."

"Excuse me, but I'm not aware of any productivity increases," Trapezoid said to Bob Arnold.

"We were saving the good news, George." Bob Arnold nodded for me to continue.

"Workers in Production, Maintenance, and Shipping hit their targets last month, with production workers combining to exceed budget on more than 30 occasions. Based on a 5-machine, 6-day, 3-shift schedule, that means the Production Department was over budget more than 8 percent of the time."

"It's been a while since that happened," Bob interjected.

"You attribute that blip to Boyle's Club?" No one spoke. "What would your record keeper do?" Trapezoid asked.

I explained that I wanted the record keeper to track and record the points the employees earned, post the results, take minutes at the monthly subcommittee meetings and the monthly Oversight Committee meetings, and generally be available when employees had questions or comments about points.

You actually believe your people will come to these meetings? On their own time?" Trapezoid spoke with such dripping sarcasm that I began to develop a dislike for the man. "And, that they'll use some initiative to accomplish something at these subcommittees? On their own time?"

I looked to Bob Arnold for his silent affirmation that I should answer, then: "I think you're selling our employees short. Not only are they interested in making the 100 Club work, but we have people waiting in line to serve on the 100 Club subcommittees."

Shaking his head and still in an obvious state of disbelief, Trapezoid waved at me, "Go ahead. Hire your record keeper. But make sure she's part-time. And, those production results better not be bullshit, Boyle."

When the first month's scores were tallied, we posted them on the bulletin boards in the canteen area and near each time clock. This scorecard contained the names of each employee and the points scored that month. In ensuing months, the scorecard included the number of points received that month and the employee's total points tallied to date. The part-time record keeper's position was called 100 Club Administrator. He did most of the scut work.

REPORT CARDS

Six months into the 100 Club's first year, it seemed we should revitalize our employees and generate more enthusiasm for the 100 Club. That's when I got the idea to use "report cards."

The report cards included a line-by-line listing of all point categories. On it, I listed the maximum number of points the employee could have received, and the total number of points an employee still could receive if he or she continued along their present course. Also, I added personal comments to each report card, such as "Keep up the good work!"; "Great cooperation!"; "What's happened to you?" And I personally signed each and every one. Then, we mailed the report cards to each employee's home address.

The day after employees received their report cards in the mail, they came to work acting like school children — and I don't mean that in a derogatory or facetious way. They gathered in small groups or one-on-one, comparing not grades, but points scored. It was great to watch.

Almost immediately, we received cost-saving ideas from two groups: The first group consisted of younger employees who still lived at home with their parents. Their suggestion went something like this: "When I got home from work, my father had already opened my mail because he saw it was from Diamond and he thought it might be important. I caught hell from him when he saw how many days of work I missed! The next time you want to report on how we are doing, why not save the company postage and hand the report cards out with the paychecks?"

The second group consisted of workers whose spouses had opened the mail and were aggravated — to put it mildly. Everybody in the house saw how much money had been lost because their husbands or wives had been absent for so many days. Further, many of the absences were unknown to their spouses. This group submitted similar cost-saving suggestions: "Save postage for the company. Hand out the report cards at work!"

Report cards continued to be sent to employees' homes, every quarter. After all, if the work ethic begins at home — and I believe it does — the involvement of an employee's family is sure to produce a win-win outcome.

WORKING WITH THE UNION

While most of the union employees reacted skeptically to the idea that management was beginning to recognize them for their good work habits, the nonunion employees — quality auditors, payroll clerks, secretaries, purchasing agents, customer service representatives, sales people — seemed to take the 100 Club more in stride.

The union's point of view was pretty well wrapped up by Stella Antowicz when Bob Arnold first introduced the 100 Club to the employees. Every benefit they had received since the United Paperworkers International Union gained bargaining power in the Palmer plant came as a result of a hard-fought negotiating process. The 100 Club was the first exception.

In contrast, nonunion employees were accustomed to dealing one-on-one with their supervisors. They underwent salary reviews on an annual basis, and most attended the traditional company-paid outings and parties. Based on their experience, the nonunion employees weren't as skeptical about the 100 Club as their union counterparts. It was good to see everybody's names, both union and nonunion, up on the 100 Club monthly score board.

One day, I read an article in a Bureau of National Affairs publication. The Labor Management Cooperative Program of the Federal Mediation and Conciliation Service (FMCS) was seeking ways to improve the relationship between management and labor in union settings. Because I thought the 100 Club was ideal, I forwarded a proposal.

As a result, Diamond International Corporation (what Bob Arnold called "New York") received a $37,500 grant to use the Palmer plant as a "model" for the expansion of the 100 Club Employee Recognition System into the three other plants in the division — Mississippi, California, and New York. The money would be used to pay for record keepers, travel expenses, and miscellaneous office expenses. The only condition of the grant mandated the hiring of an independent consultant to review the results being reported and to conduct their own employee attitudinal survey at the end of the study, which was scheduled to last two years. The results of this survey are included in the last chapter of this book.

BROADER IMPLICATIONS OF THE IDEA

One morning in October, not wanting to miss the New England foliage bursting forth with the most intense oranges and reds we had seen in years, I went for a hike to Goat's Peak in Mount Tom State Reservation, not far from home. Some of the oak and ash had already begun to lose their leaves. The pathways were covered. Below was the Connecticut River Valley, marked by church spires and factory smokestacks. In the distance, Route 90, the Massachusetts Turnpike, cut through the hills beyond which was Palmer and the Diamond plant. The view was beautiful.

Although still early, the temperature had already hit 60. I tried to keep up my pace as I hiked up the grade, but I had to slow down and finally stop to catch my breath and take in the view. I leaned against a birch tree.

I had hoped I could see the Diamond plant from up there. The previous Thursday we had received the Federal Mediation $37,500 grant. I photocopied the check and pinned it to my bulletin board. I was exhilarated. I had accomplished a significant achievement, and I knew it. The implications of the 100 Club's success, to me, to Diamond, to America, were crystal clear. Was I getting carried away? No, I told myself. You are dead-on, Danny!

How fundamental, how universal, were the "people problems" we were dealing with at Diamond. Absenteeism. Morale. Business efficiencies. Quality consciousness. Teamwork. Already the 100 Club was recording tremendous results. Attendance was improved. Productivity was up. Quality complaints were down. "Teamwork" was a damn war cry at the plant.

Why does American business squander millions of dollars chasing complicated solutions to "people problems" when the real solutions are so simple? All the symposia, all the business schools' yahoo, all the political posturing and lip-service about work ethic, all the condemnation of the U.S. labor force's capacity, education, motivation, values — it all seemed to be nothing more than self-serving fraud. It was all a lot of malarkey.

"It's all a bunch of malarkey," I said aloud, sounding much like my father.

The results being generated by the Palmer plant's 100 Club indicated nothing more than what one can expect by showing personal respect for others. "Say 'Thank you' to those who work hard for you," I could almost hear my mother say.

Staring down at my hometown that morning, I was angry. Before I knew it, I was wiping tears from my cheeks and hyperventilating. I retched, like some drunk teenager with the dry heaves.

"Nothing!" I spit. "Management has no stake in the action. They don't give a damn. They don't have to give a damn! Stockholders have a stake, it's their capital. Labor has a stake, their families depend on it." I was yelling quite loudly at the trees. "But guys like George Trapezoid have less riding on U.S. productivity than Gorbachev!"

Where did that come from, I wondered? I started to laugh at the lunacy of Gorbachev having a stake in U.S. productivity. Still, I was bitter, at that moment. Then out of the corner of my eye, I saw six, maybe eight little people, dressed in brown, each wearing a little hat, all standing in a row. They were looking at me from maybe 20 yards off the path, standing in a field of yellow maple leaves. And then I saw the adult, a very serious man. He moved, not toward me, but sideways, inching between me and the Girl Scouts, or Campfire Girls, or whatever they were. He had a stick in his right hand which he gently tapped in his left palm.

He probably thought I suffered from Tourette's syndrome. Who knows what he thought? But it was a valuable and timely reality check for me. "Don't go trying to extrapolate too much about the 100 Club, Danny Boy. What seems crystal-clear to you may be syrup to others. Keep your analysis to yourself and let the hard data compile. See what the 100 Club produces over the mid-term."

"Hi," I said to the little people. "I thought I was alone. Didn't mean to frighten you." I did a head-over-heals back flip from a standing position, which is one of my exercises. I made a perfect landing, for which I was grateful, and threw my hands in the air. All the little people smiled, some clapped. Even the adult smiled.

"Gotta go, now," I said. "Bye, bye." And off I skipped down the path, back home, to rake my backyard.

LONG-TERM RESULTS

Just two and one-half years after I joined the management team at the Palmer plant, the distrust and anger that separated management and labor had been neutralized so dramatically that the employees (represented by the United Paperworkers International Union) voted to forgo a 7.3 percent pay increase because of mutual concerns about the competition. Labor leaders told *Time* magazine they credited "Dan Boyle and the 100 Club with keeping the company afloat and for fostering a new atmosphere of cooperation with management."

During the third year on the management team at the Palmer plant, the parent company, Diamond International, was thrown into total chaos. British financier Sir James Goldsmith effected a hostile takeover of Diamond International. Subsequently, he ordered the divestiture of the corporation's operating divisions. The long-dreaded threats to close the Palmer plant seemed to be on the verge of materializing.

It was at that time I invited plant manager Bob Arnold to join me in purchasing the Palmer plant. We successfully organized a 100 percent leveraged buyout of the Palmer operation, thereby saving the jobs of over 350 individuals living in the Connecticut River Valley, including our own.

Financial institutions stood ready to lend Bob Arnold and me the money for the transaction largely due to the success credited to the 100 Club and its ability to credit meaningful common objectives between management and our employees.

During the next few years, the 100 Club Employee Recognition System popped up in over 100 corporations and organizations. Across the land, management teams discovered that implementing a 100 Club Employee Recognition System had an immediate, measurable, and positive effect on every available productivity index as well as on the overall organizational spirit.

They proved that any organization can install the 100 Club Employee Recognition System quickly and inexpensively. Also, they proved the 100 Club Employee Recognition System should be installed not by expensive outside consultants, but by the very people within the organization who make things work.

Time magazine picked up on the idea. They described the 100 Club Employee Recognition System as a "disarmingly simple formula for success." That analysis is absolutely correct. I believe it works wherever it is installed because it is simple to design, simple to communicate, simple to administer, and simple to measure. The 100 Club Employee Recognition System is a "disarmingly simple" idea whose time has come.

Recently, I addressed the annual convention of the Paper Industry Managers Association. I began my remarks by asking this:

> When was the last time you or one of your management people went around and thanked each and every employee for doing a good job? For such things as coming to work when scheduled, and on time? For working safely? For working cooperatively? For being quality-conscious? When was the last time every single one of your employees was thanked for doing a good job? Was it today? Yesterday? Last week? Last month? How about last year?

Conversely, when was the last time one of your employees was disciplined? For such things as absenteeism? For tardiness? For poor work habits? For making quality mistakes? Was it today? Yesterday? Last week? Last year?

Judging from the heads nodding and the sidelong glances from one person to another, it was obviously easier for those paper industry managers to remember instances of disciplinary action than to remember instances of praising their employees for doing a good job. Unfortunately, that's the way it is in organization after organization throughout America.

In my view, as soon as management openly rejects this pervasive and debilitating form of workplace denial, the United States of America will experience an extraordinary upsurge in productivity, corporate profits, and standards of living. What we have learned through years of experience with 100 Club Employee Recognition Systems is this: *Thanks* means millions to management. When we say "Thank you" to our employees, productivity goes through the ceiling. Recognition from within the organization is more important to employees than money.

HOW THE 100 CLUB WORKS

How does the 100 Club Employee Recognition System work? When we drive our automobiles along the same route to work every day, sometimes our minds drift off and we start thinking about a meeting tomorrow or about a problem yesterday. Before we know it, we are parked in our designated parking spot at our place of business and we can't remember driving the last three miles if our lives depended on it. Driving on automatic pilot, we accomplish our route by rote.

To some degree or another, this happens to millions of employees every day. As many of us cross over the threshold to work, our minds switch to automatic pilot. Whatever we contribute to the organization on that day is a result of rote.

The 100 Club Employee Recognition System gets employees to switch off automatic pilot and concentrate on daily tasks *by turning the workplace into a "game" with a series of specific, announced, widely known objectives.* Most important, all employees know they can achieve the objectives of the 100 Club Employee Recognition System.

Unlike incentive programs that often drive employees to the wall to achieve improbable goals, the 100 Club Employee Recognition System rewards employees when their performance reaches the *mean,* that is, the *average.* Incentive programs tend to create extreme peaks and valleys in performance. The 100 Club Employee Recognition System says "Thank you" to the average employee for average performance by calling attention to his or her ordinary contributions to the organization. As a result, the 100 Club Employee Recognition System greatly *reduces the dips* in performance, while slowly and incrementally it *builds up the mean* of performance. Hence, installing the 100 Club Employee Recognition System results in an explosion in productivity.

2

How to Install the 100 Club
in Any Organization

In this chapter, I outline facts. I learned what I know about the 100 Club Employee Recognition System from two sources: First, I created the 100 Club and implemented it at the Palmer plant in 1981 (and at Palmer's three "sister" plants between 1981 and 1983); second, I compared notes with more than 120 other managers and human resource people who implemented 100 Clubs at their locations.

MANAGEMENT'S EXPECTATIONS FOR SUCCESS

In order for the 100 Club Employee Recognition System to succeed, top management needs to understand the following postulates.

- 100 Clubs work in any organization, regardless of the size or type of goods or services it provides.

- 100 Clubs require a simple installation process, the details of which are described in this chapter.

- 100 Clubs require a commitment from management to share certain basic information with their employees.

- 100 Clubs are not a quick fix. Management should be prepared to make a long-term commitment. Management cannot stop saying "Thank you" to employees without some repercussions.

- 100 Clubs require that only objective measurements be used for rewarding points. Management must neutralize the appearance and the reality of awarding points based on subjective judgments of supervisors.

- 100 Clubs will not work as an incentive program. It will fail if management tries to use the 100 Club to make employees work harder or faster for the same pay. Employees will work harder for the same pay, but attention to work and increased productivity are only by-products of the employee recognition system.

- 100 Clubs need the top-management figure to be the chief "cheerleader." The 100 Club is not saying "Thank you" to employees for doing a good job. The *organization,* as personified by the top-management figure, is saying "Thank you" to employees.

- 100 Clubs need to be tailored to each organization by the on-site management team and employees themselves. An organization cannot simply copy the structure of another organization's 100 Club and expect it to work. 100 Clubs only work when they are designed to support management goals and employee expectations that are workplace specific.

SAYING "THANK YOU" IN THE LANGUAGE OF POINTS

The 100 Club Employee Recognition System helps top management say "Thank you" to average employees for average performance by calling attention to their ordinary day-in, day-out contributions to the organization. Employees receive points for consistently doing what they are expected to do.

The organization awards nominally priced gifts to employees based on the number of points they accrue. Typically, upon accruing the first 100 points, an employee receives a "100 Club" jacket. Additional gifts are awarded in 50-point increments thereafter.

Monthly scorecards, listing each employee's name, points received in the current period for specific activities, and accumulated points received, are posted throughout the workplace. Quarterly "report cards," mailed to each employee's home, list the points the individual received during the current period for specific activities and the accumulated points earned.

Out of this, the *language of points* evolves and permeates the organization's culture. The language of points creates a bond among employees. All employees speak the same language of points; all employees play on the same team.

However hokey or silly receiving points from top management may seem from outside an organization, within an organization the language of points grows like yeast. It is the language of points that translates the workplace into an arena in which employees play a "game" — a game with a series of specific, announced, widely known objectives.

THE POINT FORMULA CHART

The first step in installing the 100 Club Recognition System is to design a point formula. Communicating exactly how many points an employee receives for each daily activity is the job of the Point Formula Chart. It is the centerpiece of the 100 Club Employee Recognition System.

Typically, top management designs a first draft Point Formula Chart for the organization. Later, key employees are invited to join a 100 Club Management-Employee Planning Committee, which creates the final draft Point Formula Chart for the organization.

In creating the first draft Point Formula Chart, the number of points management allocates for any one individual effort should be weighted to support the existing organizational goals and objectives. The number of points management allocates for reaching any one department/team effort should be weighted to support the existing departmental/team targets and measurements.

THE POINT FORMULA DESIGN SESSION

Here are the nuts and bolts of how a successful 100 Club design session should be run.

1. The CEO calls a meeting of managers for the purpose of designing an employee recognition system. The CEO and all department/function managers attend the meeting.

2. The CEO outlines what the organization generally hopes to achieve by installing an employee recognition system and asks for everyone's cooperation. After introducing someone (typically someone from the organization; typically the human resources manager) who will be the facilitator, the CEO takes a seat in the back of the room to participate as a peer.

3. The facilitator establishes that all in attendance are part of a "design group" that is going to create an employee recognition system for their organization called the 100 Club.

IDENTIFYING THE LIST OF ACTIVITIES

First, the facilitator explains that the design group will identify certain employee activities that have a positive impact on the operations of the organization. The design group does this because top management wants to start saying "Thank you" to each employee by calling attention to his or her ordinary daily contributions to the organization.

The facilitator asks the design group to write down answers to two questions:

QUESTION ONE:
What activities are your employees, as individuals, doing now for which you think they deserve recognition?

QUESTION TWO:
What activities are happening now somewhat infrequently in your workplace (department/teamwide or organizationwide) which you would like to see happen on a more regular basis?

As the members of the design team write their answers, the facilitator sets up a large flipchart for collecting the answers to the questions. Someone reads them aloud as the facilitator writes them down, in random order.

The facilitator then asks the design group to delete certain activities from the list:

- Delete any activity that management cannot objectively measure.

- Then delete any activity that management is not currently tracking.

The end result of this process, the facilitator points out, is a list of highly rated activities that the organization can both *objectively measure and track without increasing management paperwork or administrative cost.*

Top management wants to say "Thank you" to each employee for successfully accomplishing these highly rated activities, the facilitator restates. Each time an employee successfully completes a highly rated activity, management says "Thank you" by giving him or her a specific number of points. When an employee receives 100 points, he or she becomes a member of the 100 Club and is rewarded.

DESIGNING THE POINT FORMULA CHART.

The facilitator announces that the next step is to develop a Point Formula Chart that communicates exactly how many points an employee receives for accomplishing each highly rated activity. Of course, the design group should feel free to assign more points to those activities that most directly support department/teamwide or organizationwide objectives.

When designing the Point Formula Chart, the design team must keep in mind the following two rules:

1. To maximize the effectiveness of the 100 Club Employee Recognition System, 30 percent of all employees must reach the 100-point plateau in the first nine months.

2. In order to guarantee that 30 percent of all employees earn 100 points within the first nine months, every employee must be eligible to receive a *maximum* of 140 to 160 points in the first nine months.

The facilitator tapes the list of highly rated activities to the wall and writes the following words across the top of a new sheet of flipchart paper:

"First Draft" Point Formula Chart for XYZ Organization		
Activity	**Points/Frequency**	**Maximum Points in 9 Months**

The facilitator then explains that employees earn points in three categories: through individual effort, department/team effort, and organizationwide effort. The facilitator lists the categories in the Activity column:

Activity	**Points/Frequency**	**Maximum Points in 9 Months**
Individual effort		
Department/team effort		
Organizationwide/plantwide effort		

The facilitator asks the design group to select all the highly rated activities that require only *individual effort*. As the group calls out activities, the facilitator writes them down. The group prioritizes, combines, and deletes various highly rated activities in order to streamline the list to six to ten of the most important.

Once the design group determines the six to ten activities that require only individual effort, the facilitator establishes that each employee must have the opportunity to earn a *maximum* of 84 to 96 points through his or her individual effort during the first nine months.

To avoid any possible appearance of managerial favoritism, it is important to assess points equally for every individual employee.

To sustain every employee's interest in earning points, it is important that the frequency of point distribution be well thought out.

The facilitator tells the design group to assign the number of points per frequency period that an employee can earn through individual effort in the first nine months for each highly rated activity. (See sample.)

Activity	Points/Frequency	Maximum Points in 9 Months
Individual effort (limit: 6 to 10 activities)		
100% attendance	3 per month	27
100% punctuality	2 per month	18
No lost time/accidents	20 per 9 months	20
No discipline	15 per 9 months	15
Active participation in organization committees	5 per 9 months	5
Safety suggestions	1 as accepted	—
Cost-saving suggestions	2 as implemented	—
Total maximum points available through individual effort (maximum 84 to 96 points per 9 months)		**85**

Next, the facilitator asks the design group to select all the highly rated activities that depend only on *department/team* efforts. As the group calls out the activities, the facilitator writes them down. The group then prioritizes, combines, and deletes various highly rated activities to streamline the list to four to five of the most important.

During the first nine months each employee must have the opportunity to earn a *maximum* of 42 to 48 points through his or her department/team efforts.

The facilitator explains that if an employee within a department/team has a unique job, then he or she should be able to receive points for individual effort within the department/team, even if the department/team as a whole may not achieve its highly rated activities. These points, however, cannot exceed the total department/team points available to anyone else.

The facilitator tells the design group to assign the number of points per frequency period that an employee can earn through department/team effort in the first nine months for each highly rated activity. (Two samples follow.)

Activity	Points/Frequency	Maximum Points in 9 Months
Department/team *Shipping department* effort (limit: 2 to 4 activities)		
Housekeeping	2 per month	18
No equipment damage	1 per month	9
Within overtime-hours budget	2 per month	18
Total maximum points available through Shipping department effort (maximum 42 to 48 points per 9 months)		**45**
Department/team *Maintenance department* effort (limit: 2 to 4 activities)		
Housekeeping	2 per month	18
Unscheduled machine downtime under budget	9 per quarter	27
Total maximum points available through Maintenance department effort (maximum 42 to 48 points per 9 months)		**45**

Finally, the facilitator asks the design group to select all the highly rated activities that depend only on organizationwide/ plantwide effort. As the group calls out the activities, the facilitator writes them down. The group then prioritizes, combines, and deletes various highly rated activities to streamline the list to one or two of the most important.

During the first nine months each employee must have the opportunity to earn a *maximum* of 14 to 16 points through the organizationwide/plantwide effort.

The facilitator tells the design group to assign the number of points per frequency period that an employee can earn through organizationwide/plantwide effort in the first nine months for each highly rated activity. (Sample follows.)

Activity	Points/Frequency	Maximum Points in 9 Months
Organizationwide/plantwide effort (limit:1 or 2 activities)		
Attendance meets preestablished goals	3 per quarter	9
All information on time to 100 Club administrator	2 per quarter	6
Total maximum points available through Organizationwide effort (maximum 14 to 16 points per 9 months)		**15**

The facilitator invites the design group to sit back and review its accomplishments up to that point. As time goes on, the group may add new objectively measured activities or delete existing activities as long as monitoring the activities does not increase administrative costs. Also, the point availability must remain within the preestablished formula.

The facilitator introduces a discussion about how to avoid the misconception among employees that the 100 Club Employee Recognition System is an incentive program. The discussion also focuses on how to avoid the misconception among unions that the 100 Club is a challenge to their position.

The CEO thanks everyone for participating and reminds the group that they have created only a first draft Point Formula Chart. The final draft Point Formula Chart will not be set until the employees offer their input.

The CEO instructs the facilitator to make copies of the first draft Point Formula Chart and distribute it to all managers that afternoon. Managers need to think about the highly rated activities until they meet the following week to draw up the implementation detail for gathering and reporting the necessary information to the 100 Club administrator.

• S A M P L E •

First-Draft Point Formula Chart for XYZ Organization

Activity	Points/Frequency	Maximum Points in 9 Months
Individual effort (limit: 6 to 10 activities)		
100% attendance	3 per month	27
100% punctuality	2 per month	18
No lost time/accidents	20 per 9 months	20
No discipline	15 per 9 months	15
Active participation in organization committees	5 per 9 months	5
Safety suggestions	1 as accepted	—
Cost-saving suggestions	2 as implemented	—
Total maximum points available through individual effort (maximum 84 to 96 points per 9 months)		**85**
Department/team *Production department* effort (limit: 2 to 4 activities)		
Housekeeping	2 per month	18
Meet budgeted efficiency standard	7 per shift/ per quarter	21
Set new efficiency record	5 per shift	5
Total maximum points available through Production department effort		**44**

Activity	Points/Frequency	Maximum Points in 9 Months
Department/team *Maintenance department* effort (limit: 2 to 4 activities)		
Housekeeping	2 per month	18
Unscheduled machine Downtime under budget	9 per quarter	27
Total maximum points available through Maintenance department effort (maximum 42 to 48 points per 9 months)		**45**
Department/team *Shipping department* effort (limit: 2 to 4 activities)		
Housekeeping	2 per month	18
No equipment damage	1 per month	9
Within overtime-hours budget	2 per month	18
Total maximum points available through Shipping department effort (maximum 42 to 48 points per 9 months)		**45**
Department/team *Administrative department* effort (limit: 2 to 4 activities)		
Housekeeping	2 per month	18
All monthly overhead within budget	1 per month	9
Timeliness of assignments	2 per month	18
Total maximum points available through Administrative department effort (maximum 42 to 48 points per 9 months)		**45**

Activity	Points/Frequency	Maximum Points in 9 Months
Organizationwide/plantwide effort (limit: 1 or 2 activities)		
Attendance meets preestablished goals	3 per quarter	9
All information on time to 100 Club administrator	2 per quarter	6
Total maximum points available through Organizationwide efforts		**15**

(maximum 14 to 16 points per 9 months)

• S A M P L E •

XYZ Organization — Point Formula Chart Subtotals:

In the first 9 months, the maximum number of points an employee working in the Production department is able to receive is as follows:

Individual effort	85
Any one department/team effort	44
Organizationwide effort	15
Total number	**144**

IMPLEMENTATION-DETAIL MEETING

Soon after the Point Formula design session, the CEO, facilitator, and managers should meet to review and fine-tune the Point Formula Chart. In addition, they review each highly rated activity listed on the Point Formula Chart for ability to measure and monitor it. Here is an example of a highly rated activity that is often listed on a Point Formula Chart, together with a typical example of implementation detail:

Individual Effort

Safety/
involved in no mishaps   (7 points per quarter)

Source:
Biweekly mishap reports

Person responsible for report:
Department manager

Procedures:
Department manager includes written mishap report(s) as an agenda item at biweekly managers meeting. After the meeting, copies of the report(s) are forwarded to the 100 Club administrator before being filed in the involved employee's personnel file.

Basis:
Absence of involvement in mishap in any quarter is awarded with seven (7) 100 Club Employee Recognition System points.

10-WEEK TIMETABLE FOR SETTING UP THE 100 CLUB

As soon as possible after the design session, management introduces a formalized timetable. This 10-week timetable worked very well at Diamond's Palmer plant and, subsequently, at many other sites. It is important to share this with union personnel or key employee representatives in order to promote the program and generate enthusiasm at the start.

10-Week Timetable for Setting Up the 100 Club

Wk#	Outreach	Behind the Scenes
1.	Post first sign: "The 100 Club is Coming!"; Share the idea with union representative or key employee and ask him/her to keep the "secret."	Review design session; Focus on setting specific targets and measurements for these targets; Keep from answering employees' questions with direct answers; Try to keep employees "guessing."
2.	Keep assuring employees The 100 Club is going to be a positive force in their lives, but remain vague on the specifics.	Continue to focus on targets; Think about which "key" employees you want to invite to be on planning committee.
3.	Post second sign: "No Strings Attached to the 100 Club;" Select employee members for the planning committee; Fill them in on some of the basics of the system, but keep most details for the actual meeting next week; Make sure the appropriate union representative and a "Mikey" are on committee.	Get ready for first management-employee planning meeting; Draft outline of targets – just enough to get people talking; Review Handout #1.
4.	Meet with employees and give them a draft of the first categories; Follow the theories outlined in Handout #1 — concentrate on "recognition;" Ask employees to generate discussions with co-workers and be ready to report back to the joint committee in Week 6; Solicit suggestions for new signs; Ask for more categories to add to the original outline.	Select department managers to participate in planning meeting.
5.	Continue to generate discussion in workplace; Be more specific in answers; Refer employees to planning committee members.	Continue to work on measurements and specific targets for next planning session.

Wk#	Outreach	Behind the Scenes
6.	Conduct second joint planning session; Listen to employee input and include their ideas when possible; Get more specific with your own targets; Finalize the plan; Make the final plan available to as many employees as possible to get more feedback; Consider posting the final plan on bulletin boards.	Work on recordkeeping plan.
7.	Post request for departmental subcommittees; Circulate Handout #2 describing role of subcommittees; Set meeting of subcommittees for next week.	Continue working on recordkeeping plan.
8.	Meet with subcommittees to explain their role; Have management members present; Talk about jackets and gifts; Describe how points will be recorded, by whom, and who to go to with questions.	Work on booklet detailing 100 Club system; Arrange for jacket and gift samples to be available on Kickoff Day.
9.	Clear up any lingering confusion; Post new signs; Answer outstanding questions.	Finalize script for Kickoff; Finalize recordkeeping system.
10.	Describe 100 Club system to employees in shiftwide meetings; Begin recording points.	Arrange for department managers and supervisors to attend Kickoff session.

THE ORGANIZATIONAL STRUCTURE OF A 100 CLUB

The design group should create a volunteer-based organizational structure composed of employees and managers to oversee the 100 Club Employee Recognition System.

Certain key employees should be invited to participate in the 100 Club Management-Employee Planning Committee. If a union is part of the organization, the appropriate representative should be invited to be on this committee. Also, an employee who usually is a detractor, the thorn in your side — a "Mikey" (i.e., "If Mikey likes it, we like it") — should be invited to be on the committee.

At the initial meeting of the 100 Club Management-Employee Planning Committee the first draft Point Formula Chart is introduced. From the beginning, employee members should be encouraged to analyze, criticize, and improve the Point Formula Chart. Management is frequently surprised by the objectivity and caliber of employee input at this stage.

At the same initial meeting of the 100 Club Management-Employee Planning Committee, distribute "An Invitation to Participate in the 100 Club Planning Committee" (see Handout #1).

RESPONSIBILITIES

A few weeks before launching a 100 Club, post and circulate "The 100 Club Committee Responsibilities" (Handout #2) to everyone. It describes the purpose of the 100 Club department/team subcommittees and the 100 Club Oversight Committee.

Handout #1

An Invitation to Participate in the 100 Club Planning Committee

All too often, the only employees who receive attention from management are those whose work habits have negative impact on the efficiency and productivity of our organization. The so-called "attention-grabbers" have been those who received a "talking-to" for their absenteeism, inattention to the task at hand, carelessness, etc. The list is endless.

But, what about the "good" employees? Shouldn't we, as managers, be giving the majority of our attention to those employees who make an organization successful?

The 100 Club is designed to do just that — recognize the positive! It rewards those employees who do a good job day after day, year after year. It never fails to call attention to those employees whose work habits have a good impact on our organization.

[Here, list some of the highly rated activities the design team
included on the Point Formula Chart.]

These are the same things you, as employees, have done for as long as you've worked for us. Unfortunately, we have taken you and many of your achievements for granted. We are no longer going to take you for granted!

This system isn't just a one-way street. In order to be successful, we need the help of each employee. We have asked you to participate on this 100 Club Management-Employee Planning Committee. Over the next few weeks, we will be meeting a number of times to plan for our 100 Club.

After today's session, you have two weeks to discuss our ideas with your co-workers. We urge you to report back to us during the week of _____ to offer your suggestions.

As we move through this implementation process, we will continue to keep you posted. The 100 Club is scheduled to be kicked off during the week of _____. We will be posting more information as we move closer to that date.

Remember, this system is new to our organization. If it has flaws, we can — and will — correct them. The main factor is this: the 100 Club is for the employee whose relationship with our organization has been and continues to be a positive ingredient in our success.

The 100 Club is our way of saying: **"Thanks, for a job well done!"**

Handout #2

The 100 Club Committee Responsibilities

It would be virtually impossible to expect the 100 Club system to operate without questions, disagreements, disputes or legitimate concerns. In anticipation of these things, subcommittees will be formed to represent employees in each department.

This and other notices are posted throughout the organization as a call for volunteers to serve on these subcommittees. Each subcommittee will consist of *no more than five (5) employees,* if possible. If the respective department is small, then three (3) employees may be enough for that subcommittee. Contact your department/team manager to volunteer to serve on a 100 Club subcommittee.

The purpose of each subcommittee is to serve as a line of communication between the respective department/team employees and the 100 Club Oversight Committee. Subcommittee members solicit questions/comments from co-workers, discuss these concerns at monthly department/team meetings and report on these items to the 100 Club Oversight committee.

The 100 Club Oversight Committee will consist of equal numbers of management representatives and employee representatives, preferably no more than four (4) from each group. Employee representatives on the 100 Club Oversight Committee will be selected by their department/team subcommittee, each of which will be allowed no more than one (1) representative.

The 100 Club Oversight Committee will meet on a monthly basis and is responsible for answering questions and settling disputes with regard to all aspects of the 100 Club.

Once the 100 Club Oversight Committee makes a decision, it provides the results to each subcommittee which, in turn, reports to department/team members. Any employee who has a question concerning point allocations, status of cost-saving suggestions, etc., should refer the question to his or her department/team subcommittee.

In selecting the chairperson for the 100 Club Oversight Committee, it is suggested that the designation be determined by majority vote of all members of the 100 Club Oversight Committee, with the position alternating between management and employee representatives, and that each term last for three (3) successive months.

[N.B.: If your organization is unionized, be sure that Handout #2 states that the union president or other appropriate union representative is a *de facto* member of the Oversight Committee.]

SAMPLE 100 CLUB ORGANIZATION CHART

It is, of course, always healthy to have an organization chart pinned to the wall, so anyone who wants to challenge it may do so. I've taken a lot of ribbing about my first 100 Club Organization Chart. At the Palmer plant, Bob Arnold's secretary, Julie Strempek, got so excited about the 100 Club and employee involvement, she drew up this organization chart at home one night. I think it's perfect. At least, it was appropriate and effective for the Palmer plant.

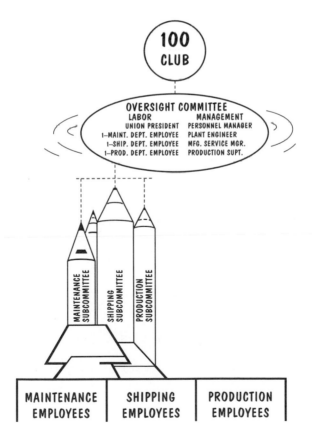

THE 100 CLUB ADMINISTRATOR

It is a good idea to have the part-time 100 Club Administrator in place so he or she can attend the initial Point Formula design session. Here is a sample job description for the position:

---

100 Club Administrator Job Description

1. Attends all meetings of the Oversight Committee and the subcommittees. Takes notes at each meeting and makes copies of notes available to each person in attendance. (Notes of meetings may be posted on bulletin boards — at discretion of Oversight Committee.)

2. Maintains up-to-date records of points received by each employee, and is available to answer questions from employees as well as members of management pertaining to point distribution.

3. Coordinates the reporting of points with each department and is liaison between departments and the CEO.

4. Tracks cost-saving suggestions employees hand in and submits these suggestions to the Oversight Committee. Further, reports back to employee regarding status of suggestions.

5. Prepares monthly reports for CEO on progress and results of 100 Club.

6. Develops signs, charts, etc., to be hung in visible locations throughout the organization to maintain employee interest and enthusiasm.

7. Assists in the development of handbook, detailing point categories, targets, etc. for the 100 Club.

8. Prepares and posts monthly point tallies for all employees.

9. Prepares "report cards," as necessary, and coordinates mailing them with appropriate management representatives.

10. Coordinates purchases of jackets and gifts, and arranges presentation ceremonies to include CEO.

3

Sample Designs of 100 Club Implementations

Organizations with 100 Clubs are as varied as public and private organizational management in general. They include small and large service companies; professional groups; large manufacturing companies; government agencies; colleges and universities, and so on.

Following is a selection of implementation materials developed by seven different organizations. Although the details are real, I substituted names for the organizations.

AARDVARK APPLIANCE, INC.

Organizations that provide customers with individual creativity, diagnostic skills, and efficiency have been terrific at designing simple and effective 100 Clubs that work for their organizations.

Managers of software development firms, medical rescue teams, day-care centers, travel agencies, automobile repair shops, radio stations, advertising agencies, and the like, may approach the 100 Club with less structure and fewer measurable activities than *Fortune* 500 companies, but their solutions are often more creative.

Aardvark Appliance, Inc. is such a company. It provides 24-hour major-appliance repair services to customers in a large metropolitan area. It repairs equipment both on-site and in its shop. Customers include manufacturers (warranty work), retailers, leasing companies, institutions, and individual families. The following pages show Aardvark's Point Formula Chart, procedures and definitions, departmental categories, scorecard, and report cards.

100 Club Model Point Formula Chart for Aardvark Appliance, Inc.

Activity	Frequency	Points	9 Months
General			
Attendance	2 months	5	20
Punctuality	1 month	1	9
Safety: no mishaps	1 month	2	18
not the cause	1 month	1	9
Correct tickets	1 month	1	9
No discipline	6 months	15	15
Correct time cards	1 month	1	9
Shop			
Proper paperwork	1 months	9	9
Unscheduled overtime	3 months	7	21
Respond w/in 4 hrs.	6 months	10	10
Sales			
Timely itinerary	1 month	1	9
Item of the month	1 month	1	9
New customers	1 month	2	18
Timely trip reports	1 month	1	9
Office			
Extra assignments	1 month	3	27
Work overtime	3 months	6	18
Service			
Respond w/in 4 hrs.	6 months	10	10
No negative comments	6 months	5	5
Work overtime	3 months	1	15
Proper reports in	2 months	1	4
Contact office	2 months	2	8

Activity	Frequency	Points	9 Months
Managers			
Notify bookkeeper	3 months	5	15
Submit itinerary	2 months	3	12
On time for meetings	1 month	1	9
Perform correct job	2 months	2	8
General Manager			
Business plans OK	3 months	3	9
Consistent decisions	2 months	2	8
On time for appointments	2 months	3	8
Report whereabouts	2 month	3	12
Timely rumor board	1 month	1	9
Extras for Everyone			
Suggestions			
Made	As given	1	
Implemented	As implemented	2	
Mgr. followup	As accomplished	1	
Report quality			
problems	As reported	5	
Education/training	On completion	5	
Co. committees	9 months	5	
Upgrade skills	As accomplished	5	
Praise board	As nominated	5	
Voluntarism in community	9 months	5	
Info. to records	1 month	2	

Examples of Potential Point Totals at the 9-Month Period
(Aardvark Appliances, Inc.)

Shop		
	OK paperwork	9
	Attendance	20
	Punctuality	9
	Safety - both	27
	OK tickets	9
	No discipline	15
	OK time cards	9
	Unscheduled O/T	21
	Report w/in 4 hrs.	10
	2 suggestions	2
	1 implemented	2
	Report quality error	5
	Praise board	5
		143

Sales		
	Attendance	20
	Punctuality	9
	Safety - both	27
	Itinerary	9
	Item of month	9
	New customers	18
	Right trip reports	9
	2 suggestions	2
	1 implemented	2
	Praise board	5
	No discipline	15
		125

Office		
	Attendance	20
	Punctuality	9
	Safety – both	27
	No discipline	15
	Extra assignments	27
	Work O/T	18
	2 suggestions	2
	1 implemented	2
	Praise board	5
		125

Service	Attendance	20
	Punctuality	9
	Safety - both	27
	No discipline	15
	Report w/in 4 hrs.	10
	No negatives	5
	Work O/T	15
	Proper reports	4
	Contact office	8
	1 suggestion	1
	1 implemented	2
	Training	5
	Praise board	5
		126
Managers	Attendance	20
	Safety – both	27
	Notify bookkeeper	15
	Itinerary	12
	On time for meetings	9
	Perform job	8
	1 suggestion	1
	1 implemented	2
	1 followup	1
	Info to records	18
		121
General Manager	Attendance	20
	Safety – both	27
	Business plans	9
	Consistency	8
	On time appointments	8
	Report whereabouts	12
	Rumor board	9
	Followup suggestion	1
	Report quality problem	5
	Community service	5
	Info. to records	18
		120

100 Club Implementation Detail (Procedures and Definitions) for Aardvark Appliance, Inc.

INDIVIDUAL CATEGORIES

1. **Attendance**
   Source:
   > Individual time cards

   Person Responsible:
   > Payroll clerk

   Procedures:
   > Payroll clerk checks time cards. Absentee memos are sent to 100 Club Administrator before being filed in employee's personnel file.

2. **On time**
   Source:
   > Individual time cards

   Person responsible:
   > Payroll clerk

   Procedures:
   > Payroll clerk checks time cards. Absentee memos are sent to 100 Club administrator before being filed in employee's personnel file.

3. **Safety: Involved in no mishaps**
   Source:
   > Biweekly mishap reports

   Person responsible:
   > Department managers

   Procedures:
   > Department managers include written mishap reports as an agenda item at biweekly managers meeting. Individuals involved in any mishap are noted. After the meeting, copies of the reports are forwarded to the 100 Club Administrator before being filed in involved employee's personnel file.

4. **Safety: Responsible for no mishaps**
   Source:
   > Biweekly mishap reports

Person responsible:
Department managers
Procedures:
Department managers include written mishap reports as an agenda item at biweekly managers meeting. Individuals responsible for any mishap are noted. After the meeting, copies of the reports are forwarded to the 100 Club Administrator before being filed in the responsible employee's personnel file.

5. **Correct tickets**
Source:
Customer tickets
Person responsible:
Service manager
Procedures:
If all critical customer information is not listed on tickets, whomever received the customer call is notified of discrepancy by service manager, who sends a copy of his/her monthly tally to the 100 Club Administrator.

6. **No warnings**
Source:
Warning memos
Person responsible:
Supervisors issuing warning memo
Procedures:
Copies of warning memos are sent to 100 Club Administrator before going into personnel file.

7. **Correct time cards**
Source:
Time cards
Person responsible:
Payroll clerk
Procedures:
Incomplete information on time card will be brought to the attention of the individual employee by the payroll clerk who sends a copy of his/her monthly tally to 100 Club Administrator.

DEPARTMENTAL CATEGORIES

Shop
1. **Proper paperwork**
   Source:
   > Job billing statements

   Person responsible:
   > Billing clerk

   Procedures:
   > Improperly prepared paperwork will be brought to the attention of the individual employee by the billing clerk, who sends a copy of his/her monthly tally to 100 Club Administrator.

2. **Unscheduled overtime**
   Source:
   > Requests for overtime approval

   Person responsible:
   > Department caller

   Procedures:
   > All approved requests for overtime are satisfied by shop staffing, as reported to George and 100 Club Administrator.

3. **Respond within 4 hours**
   Source:
   > Department call sheet

   Person responsible:
   > Department caller

   Procedures:
   > Department called is able to fully staff for emergencies within 4 hours of emergency.

Sales
1. **Handing in weekly itinerary**
   Source:
   > Itinerary

   Person responsible:
   > Sales manager

Procedures:

Submitted to sales manager three days before the start of the week. If not submitted on time, notice will be sent to 100 Club Administrator.

2. **Item of the month**

Source:

Invoices

Person responsible:

Sales manager

Procedures:

Achievement of sales goals for Item of the Month is reported to 100 Club Administrator.

3. **New customers**

Source:

Approved credit applications

Person responsible:

Bookkeeper

Procedures:

Tardy expense reports will be brought to the attention of the sales department manager by the bookkeeper, who sends a copy of his/her memo to the 100 Club Administrator.

Office

1. **Extra assignments**

Source:

Requests from George

Person responsible:

Office manager

Procedures:

Completed extra assignments will be reported by office manager to 100 Club Administrator.

2. **Work overtime**
    Source:
    > Requests for overtime approval

    Person responsible:
    > Office manager

    Procedures:
    > All approved requests for overtime are satisfied by office staffing, as reported to George and 100 Club Administrator.

Service
1. **Respond within 4 hours**
    Source:
    > Job tickets

    Person responsible:
    > Service manager

    Procedures:
    > Achievement of quick response goals are reported to 100 Club Administrator.

2. **No negative comments**
    Source:
    > Follow-up calls by service manager

    Person responsible:
    > Service manager

    Procedures:
    > Achievement of no-negative-comments goals are reported to 100 Club Administrator.

3. **Work overtime**
    Source:
    > Requests for overtime approval

    Person responsible:
    > Service manager

    Procedures:
    > All approved requests for overtime are satisfied by 100% service department staffing, as reported to George and 100 Club Administrator.

4. **Proper reports in**
   Source:
   > Job tickets and vehicle reports

   Person responsible:
   > Office manager

   Procedures:
   > Monthly memo from office manager states when proper reports are in, a copy of which goes to 100 Club Administrator.

5. **Contact office**
   Source:
   > Service reps call-in sheets

   Person responsible:
   > Service manager

   Procedures:
   > Achievement of minimum-office-contact-requirement goals is reported to 100 Club Administrator.

Managers
1. **Notify bookkeeper**
   Source:
   > Bookkeeper's report log

   Person responsible:
   > Bookkeeper

   Procedures:
   > Bookkeeper maintains a log of monthly reports required from each manager. Quarterly, the bookkeeper copies the log, highlighting 100% compliance, and forwards it to 100 Club Administrator.

2. **Submit itinerary**
   Source:
   > Itineraries

   Person responsible:

   Procedures:

3. **On time for meetings**
    Source:
    > Meeting minutes

    Person responsible:
    > Meeting secretary

    Procedures:
    > Copies of minutes, including those in attendance on time, are sent to the 100 Club Administrator.

4. **Perform correct job**
    Source:

    Person Responsible:

    Procedures:

George (General Manager)
1. **Business plans OK**
    Source:
    > Quarterly business plan updates

    Person responsible:
    > George's assistant

    Procedures:
    > Copies of business plan updates are delivered to accountant by George's assistant, who records date of delivery in 100 Club records.

2. **Consistent decisions**
    Source:
    > Manager's meeting

    Person responsible:
    > George's assistant

    Procedures:
    > "Potential inconsistent management decisions" is a fixed agenda item at biweekly managers meeting. By consensus, the absence of "inconsistent decisions" for that two-week period is noted in the minutes, and recorded in 100 Club records.

3. **On time for appointments**
    Source:
    >   George's schedule
    Person responsible:
    >   George's assistant
    Procedures:
    >   Being late, without providing prior notification, to less than one appointment a week is recorded on George's schedule by the dispatcher, a copy of which is sent to the 100 Club Administrator.

4. **Report whereabouts**
    Source:
    >   George's schedule
    Person responsible:
    >   George's assistant
    Procedures:
    >   Not knowing where George is when whereabouts is required more than once a week is recorded on George's schedule by his assistant, a copy of which is sent to 100 Club Administrator,

5. **Rumor Board timely**
    Source:
    >   Rumors or questions posted on Rumor Board
    Person responsible:
    >   George's assistant
    Procedures:
    >   George's assistant makes two copies of any question posted on the rumor board not answered in 24 hours. One copy goes to the individual responsible for answering the rumor, the other copy goes to the 100 Club Administrator.

Extras for Everyone
1. **Suggestions — accepted**
    Source:
    >   Oversight Committee suggestion form
    Person responsible:
    >   Secretary of Oversight Committee

Procedures:

> All suggestions must receive 25% membership approval before forwarded to George for consideration and to 100 Club Administrator.

2. **Suggestions — implemented**
   Source:

   > Managers meeting minutes

   Person responsible:

   > George's assistant

   Procedures:

   > The managers and George select certain suggestions to be implemented. These are noted in meeting minutes, a copy of which goes to the 100 Club Administrator.

3. **Suggestions — manager follow-up**
   Source:

   > Managers meeting minutes

   Person responsible:

   > George's assistant

   Procedures:

   > Managers following up on newly implemented suggestions. They report on success or lack of success of each at meeting, which is noted in meeting minutes, a copy of which goes to 100 Club Administrator.

4. **Report quality-related problems**
   Source:

   > All employees

   Person responsible:

   > Department manager

   Procedures:

   > Problem is investigated by manager, who writes a memo to George describing the problem, the corrective action taken, and the name of the individual who reported it. A copy of the memo is sent to the 100 Club Administrator before being filed in the employee's personnel file.

5. Education/training — when accepted
    Source:
      Personal letter from individual about to receive training
    Person responsible:
      100 Club Oversight Committee chairperson
    Procedures:
      A letter describing training is sent to Oversight Committee, which
      accepts or rejects training as appropriate for 100 Club recognition.
      A copy of the letter, if approved by the Committee, is sent to 100
      Club Administrator before being filed in employee's personnel file.

6. Education/training —when completed
    Source:
      Personal letter from individual upon completion of training
    Person responsible:
      100 Club Oversight Committee Chairperson
    Procedures:
      A letter describing training completed is sent to Oversight
      Committee. Copy of the letter is sent to 100 Club Administrator
      before being filed in employee's personnel file.

7. Company committees
    Source:
      Commendation letter
    Person responsible:
      100 Club Oversight Committee
    Procedures:
      After serving on a company committee for a year, the Oversight
      Committee writes a letter of commendation to the individual
      employee, a copy of which is sent to the 100 Club Administrator
      before being filed in the employees personnel file.

8. Get new skills
    Source:
      Letter from employee describing new skill acquired.
    Person responsible:
      Secretary of 100 Club Oversight Committee

Procedures:

A manager or an individual him/herself may write a letter to the Oversight Committee describing the new skill and how it contributes to the business effort. If approved, the letter is sent to the 100 Club Administrator before being filed in employee's personnel file.

9. **Praise board**

Source:

Letter recommending praise, together with approval of Oversight Committee

Person responsible:

Secretary of 100 Club Oversight Committee

Procedures:

Any employee may write a letter to the Oversight Committee recommending praise for an individual. If approved, the letter is sent to the 100 Club Administrator before being filed in the praised employee's personnel file.

10. **Get information to 100 Club Administrator**

Source:

100 Club Administrator's log

Person responsible:

General manager or department managers

Procedures:

Occurrences of required information not arriving at 100 Club Administrator's office in a timely fashion will be noted on the 100 Club Administrator's log.

100 Club Companywide Scorecard for Aardvark Appliance, Inc.

No.	Name	Position	Points from Last Month	Attendance	On Time	Safety: Involved	Safety: Cause	Correct tickets	No warnings	Correct time cards	Department Totals	Suggestions: Accepted	Suggestions: Implemented	Suggestions: Manager follow-up	Report Quality-related problems	Education: Training when accepted	Education: Training when completed	Company committees	Get new skills	Praise board	Get info to 100 Club Administrator	Points from this month	Accumulated points
						Individual					*Dept*					*Companywide*						*Totals*	
45	Tony A.	Salesperson																					
05	Susan T.	Salesperson																					
47	Inez M.	Salesperson																					
88	Tom H.	Admin Assist																					
65	Greg C.	Admin Assist																					

Department: Shop

No.	Name	Position																					
14	Sam T.	Repairs																					
32	Lanny B.	Repairs																					
33	Pat B.	Repairs																					
52	Jan G.	Scheduler																					
04	Virginia T.	Telephone Op																					
27	Josie C.	Assist Mgr																					
77	Jeff D.	Weekend Mgr																					

Department: Office

No.	Name	Position																					
53	Murray D.	Bkpr: AP																					
78	Helen D.	Bkpr: AR																					

Quarterly 100 Club Employee "Report Card" for Aardvark Appliance, Inc.

Employee: _____

Address: _____

City, State, Zip: _____

Home Phone: _____

	Total Points Earned This Quarter	Total Bonus Points Earned This Quarter
Individual Categories		
Attendance		
On time		
Safety: Involved		
Safety: Cause		
Correct tickets		
No warnings		
Correct time cards		
Department Totals		
Extras for Everyone		
Suggestions: Accepted		
Suggestions: Implemented		
Suggestions: Manager follow-up		
Report quality-related problems		
Education: Training when accepted		
Education: Training when completed		
Company committees		
Get new skills		
Praise board		
Get info to 100 Club Administrator		
Total accumulated points earned as of the end of last quarter		
Total points earned this quarter		
Total accumulated points earned as of the end of this quarter		

QUIET-SIDE FUNERAL HOME

Privately held professional firms that provide services to the public have unique management challenges. Often they have no business plan or formalized goals. Typically, the professionals themselves have no management training.

Traditionally, private practices are run in any way necessary to support the personal goals of the "rainmakers." Often, more than one rainmaker resides at any one private clinic or law firm, each maintaining his/her own fiefdom, sometimes competing with each other for resources. Talk about a hothouse for employee alienation! This same situation holds true in most organizations run by architects, dentists, and even rabbis, priests, or ministers.

Institutionalizing a "Thank you" system for the administrative staff, or even including middle management, nurses, paralegals, or firm/clinic administrators is a no-brainer. Measurable criteria are everywhere. But for professional partners or associates to subject themselves to the rigors of a point formula and peer-to-peer review takes a special commitment from the professional.

Any professional organization without an operating plan, such as a business plan or an annual review, is not likely to do well with a 100 Club. On the other hand, professional firms with a business plan achieve an extraordinary lift from a 100 Club, both in teamwork and efficiency.

In professional firms, size in itself does not seem to be a mitigating factor in the success of a 100 Club. One small-sized operation in the Northwest is a funeral home. Following is a model Point Formula Chart for Quiet-Side Funeral Home. This is about as generic a 100 Club Point Formula as I've seen.

100 Club Model Point Formula Chart for Quiet-Side Funeral Home

Activity	Points/Frequency	Points/ 9-Months	Bonus Points	9-Month Availability
Attendance	3 pts./month	27	10	37
Punctuality	3 pts./month	27		27
No injuries	7 pts./3 months	21		21
No discipline	5 pts./3 months	15		15
Manager meets objective	5 pts./3 months	15		15
Suggestions	2 pts. when accepted			—
Suggestions	5 pts. when implemented			—
Community involvement	1 pt./3 months when accepted	3		—
Total Points Available First 9 Months				**115**

MAJOR MANUFACTURING, INC.

My personal experience with the Diamond International plants prepared me to expect great things from large manufacturing companies that commit to a 100 Club.

The implementation materials below are a terrific example of how a high-powered *Fortune* 500 company can integrate the 100 Club deep into the fabric of their operations. I was particularly impressed by their simple approach to the 100 Club definitions and reporting procedures.

100 Club Point Formula Chart for Major Manufacturing, Inc.

Individual Effort

Category	Standard	Frequency	Points/9 Months
Absenteeism	No absences	2 pts./month	18
Lateness	No lates/leave early	1 pt./month	9
Accidents	None	6 pts./month	18
Discipline	No disciplinary action	10 pts./quarter	30
Plant OSHA			
Incident rate	5.5	8 pts./year	6
Annual div.			
quality audit	80+	4 pts./year	3
Suggestions	As submitted	1/suggestion	—
Suggestions	As implemented	1/Implementation	—
Extra activities	As recorded	2 pts./activity/ 6-month period (20 pts. max./year)	—

Production

Category	Standard	Frequency	Points/9 Months
O.E. shift	95%	1/week	39
Quality review shift	80+	1/month	9
% 2nd shift	2%	1/month	9
Thru-put std. per shift	100%	1/month	9
Job eff. dept.	96%	1/month	9
Material O/U dept.	3%	1/month	9

Warehouse/Shipping

Category	Standard	Frequency	Points/9 Months
L/H per truckload	1.2	3/month	27
Shipping errors	none	2/month	18
Forklift			
inspection cards	2 misses	2/month	18
Demurrage	500	1/month	9
Material O/U	3%	1/month	9

Maintenance

Category	Standard	Frequency	Points/9 Months
O.E.	93%	1/week	58
Maint. exp. % of S.V.P.	3%	1/month	9
Preventive			
maintenance	as scheduled	1/month	9
Thru-put (std. perf.)	97%	1/month	9

100 Club Point-Tracking Procedures and Definitions
for Major Manufacturing, Inc.

I.   INDIVIDUAL CATEGORIES

A. Absenteeism: A person who does not have an excused absence for 3 months will receive the points. Excused absences will be allowed for all items listed in the employee handbook (i.e. jury duty, military, etc.) as well as a doctor's slip for medical reasons.

  3 points for 3 months

B. Tardiness: A person who does not punch in for work more than 5 minutes after scheduled time for an entire calendar month will receive the points.

  1 point for 1 month

C. Safety: A person who does not become injured seriously enough to be considered an OSHA recordable for a particular 3-calendar-month period will receive the points. No waivers are given even if the injury was caused by someone else's negligence.

  10 points for 3 months

D. Disciplinary Action: A person who does not receive any recorded warning in his/her personnel record for a period of 3 months will receive the points. A verbal warning that is recorded in a person's records will be considered disciplinary action. There can be unrecorded verbal warnings and it is the responsibility of the supervisor to inform the individual which type of warning is issued at the time it is given.

  6 points for 3 months

E. Extra Activities: There will be points given for community or plant service. These activities must be from the approved list below. Other activities can be approved after review by the committee. Each individual or his/her supervisor must certify that he has taken part in the particular activity. The supervisor will be responsible for turning the list in to the 100 Club Administrator monthly. The following is the approved activities list.

1. Blood drive
2. The individual's local fire department
3. The individual's local E.M.S.
4. 4-H Supervisor
5. Boy Scout or Girl Scout leader
6. Cancer drive
7. Heart Fund drive
8. Plant safety committee volunteer
9. Plant picnic committee
10. 100 Club committee

These points are considered bonus points: 2 points/activity
10 points maximum in a 6-month period.

F. Suggestions: Individuals will receive points for submitting suggestions to improve plant operations, environment, etc. The suggestions will be evaluated for merit and viability by a committee made up of the maintenance supervisor and approximately three plant employees. Points will be awarded on the following basis.

1.75 points if suggestion is adopted
2 points if suggestion is implemented
.25 points if suggestion is judged reasonable

Individual section reporting forms:

- Absenteeism, Tardiness, Disciplinary Action: Personnel file — Supervisors review monthly and hand in list to Administrator.
- Safety: OSHA recordable form — Plant SAS turns list in to Administrator monthly.
- Extra Activities: Supervisors turn in certified list to Administrator monthly.
- Suggestions: Supervisors will collect suggestions from box and turn them over to the 100 Club Administrator.

II. ENTIRE PLANT CATEGORIES

The following categories will give points to all employees in the plant when the objective is obtained or surpassed.

A. Quality/Corporate Quality Audit: If all products reviewed at the corporate audit obtain point evaluation of over 80 points all individuals receive that stated points:

    1 point for every quality audit

B. Quality/% Return and Allowances of Sales: If for the month, the percent R & A is .25 or below, all individuals will receive the listed points per month:

    .5 points for each month

C. Total Overuse: If for any particular month the total overuse is 1.2% or less, each individual will receive the listed points:

    .5 points for each month

D. Percent Seconds: When the entire plant average of seconds for a month is 1.6% or lower, each individual will receive the listed points:

    .5 points for each month

E. Damaged Property: When the plant property, buildings, or machinery has not been damaged or destroyed more than $500 in a 3-month period due to carelessness or negligence, all individuals will receive the listed points:

    .5 points for each month

F. Filler Efficiency: When the plant is able to use filler at a rate equal or greater than 104% efficiency, all individuals will receive the listed points:

    .5 points for each month

G. Headlap Efficiency: When the plant used enough headlap granules compared to standard that 100% of what is supposed to be used is used, each individual will receive the listed points:

    1 point for each month

Entire plant reporting forms:
- Quality Corporate Audit and % R & A: Manufacturing engineer will forward to the 100 Club Administrator the monthly R & A report and the results of the corporate audit.
- Total Overuse, % Seconds, Filler Efficiency, Headlap Efficiency: The SAS will forward monthly these numbers from the monthly reconciliation sheet.
- Damaged Property: The maintenance supervisor will forward the damaged property record sheet to the 100 Club Administrator quarterly.

III. DEPARTMENTAL CATEGORIES

Only individuals in a particular department can receive those particular points. If an individual changes departments or shifts, he/she will get the points for whichever department or shift that he/she was assigned the longest. Supervisors are responsible for notifying the 100 Club Administrator of all such changes.

A. Production Department

1. Housekeeping: On a weekly basis, the production areas will be evaluated on a predetermined criteria. If the department earns an average of 12 points for the month, each individual will receive the listed points:
      1 point for each month

2. Quality Mini-Audits: If the product evaluated has an average rating of 98 points or more, the individuals from the shift that produced the product will receive the listed points:
      1 point for each month

3. Percent Good Product: When a shift averages 93.0% good product or better, each individual on that shift will receive the listed points.
      1 point for each month

4. Percent Cross Web or Manual: When a shift runs 3.0% or less in cross web average for a month, each individual on that shift will receive the listed points:

   1 point for each month

5. Standard Performance: When a shift averages 100% standard performance for a month, each individual on that shift will receive the listed points. For every 1% above 100 on a shift monthly average, each individual on that shift will receive additional points as listed below:

   1 point for each month/
   additional .5 points for each 1% over 100%

6. Operating Efficiency: When a shift averages for a month 95.5% operating efficiency, each individual on that shift will receive the points listed:

   1 point for each month

Production Department reporting forms:
   • Quality Mini-Audit, % Good Product. % Cross Web, Standard Performance, Operating Efficiency: The manufacturing engineer will give to the 100 Club Administrator the daily production statistics worksheet and the monthly quality review forms for calculation of these points.
   • Housekeeping: Evaluation will be conducted on a weekly basis by 3 people (1 from general office, 2 from 100 Club Committee). Standard forms will be used and will be submitted weekly to the 100 Club Administrator.

B. Quality Control Department

1. Housekeeping: On a weekly basis, the quality control areas will be evaluated on a predetermined criteria. If the department earns an average of 12 points for the month, each individual will receive the listed points:

   1 point for each month

2. Tests Completed: For every two weeks that an individual com-
    pletes 87% of test requested, that individual will receive points
    listed below:
    > 1 point for every two weeks/
    > .5 points for each percent over 100%

3. Special Projects: When an individual completed 3 special
    projects in a month that are listed on the special record sheet,
    that individual will receive bonus points as listed below:
    > 1 bonus point every 3 specials/
    > maximum 1 point every month

4. Calibrations: Every month that the Quality Control Department
    completes 4 line calibrations, 1 lab equipment calibration and
    turns in maintenance repair requires ton equipment, each
    individual will receive the points listed below:
    > 1 point every month

5. Standard Performance: When the standard performance of
    the plant averages 100% for a month, each individual in the
    maintenance department will receive the points listed below.
    For every 1% above 100 based on plant monthly average, each
    individual will receive additional points as listed below:
    > 1 point per month/
    > additional .5 points for each 1% over 100%

Quality control reporting forms:
- Test Completed, Special Projects, Calibrations: The
  Manufacturing Engineer will be required to give the 100 Club
  Administrator the test completed forms, special project forms,
  and calibration records to calculate points to be awarded.
- Housekeeping: Evaluation will be conducted on a weekly
  basis on unannounced days by 3 people (1 from general office,
  2 from 100 Club Committee). Standard forms will be used and
  will be submitted weekly to the 100 Club Administrator.

C. Maintenance Department

1. Housekeeping: On a weekly basis, the maintenance areas will be evaluated on a predetermined criteria. If the department earns an average of 12 points for the month, each individual will receive the listed points:
    1 point for each month

2. Standard Performance: When the standard performance of the plant averages 100% for a month, each individual in the maintenance department will receive the points listed below. For every 1% above 100 based on plant monthly average, each individual will receive additional points as listed below:
    1 point per month/
    additional .5 points for each 1% over 100%

3. Operating Efficiency: When the operating efficiency for the entire plant averages over 95.5%, each individual in the maintenance department will receive the points listed below:
    1 point for every month

4. Maintenance Operating Efficiency: When the monthly average maintenance operating efficiency for a shift is 98% or above, each individual on that shift will receive the points listed below:
    1 point for every month

5. Maintenance Cost per Ton Produced: When the monthly average maintenance cost is $4.10 per ton produced or less, each individual in the Maintenance Department will receive the points listed below:
    1 point for every month

6. Percent Spare Parts in Stock: For every month that the spare parts review indicates that the plant has 93% or more in stock, each individual in the Maintenance Department will receive the points listed below:
    .5 points every month

Maintenance Department reporting forms:
- Housekeeping: Evaluations will be conducted on a weekly basis on unannounced days by 3 people (1 from general office, 2 from 100 Club Committee). Standard forms will be used and will be submitted weekly to the 100 Club Administrator.
- Standard Performance, Operating Efficiency, Maintenance Operating Efficiency: The manufacturing engineer will be responsible for giving to the 100 Club Administrator.
- Maintenance Cost per Ton Produced: The SAS will forward the monthly information to the 100 Club Administrator for recording and point assignment.
- Percent Spare Parts in Stock: The maintenance supervisor will report to the 100 Club Administrator the results of the monthly spare parts review for recording and point assignment.

D. Warehouse and Shipping Department

1. Housekeeping: On a weekly basis, the warehouse areas will be evaluated on a predetermined criteria. If the department earns an average of 12 points for the month, each individual will receive the listed points:
   1 point for every month

2. Labor-hours per Truckload: When the average for the month of 1.4 labor-hours per truckload is met, or lower, the entire warehouse and shipping staff will receive the points listed below:
   2 points for every month/
   2 points for every 10th (.1) below 1.4 hours

3. Service C & A's Percentage: When the service C & A's total is equal to or less than an average of 1 per operating shift a month, each individual in the department will receive the points listed. The service C & A's considered will be only for shortages, incorrect color, an incorrect product:
   .5 points for every month

4. Inventory Adjustments: When the total inventory adjustment for a quarter of a year is equal to or less than .1% reduction, each individual will receive the points listed below:
   3 points every quarter

5. Forklift Inspection Cards: Every month that an individual turns in 100% of the required forklift inspection cards, that individual will receive the points listed below:
   .5 points per month

6. Overtime: When the entire department has 2% or less overtime in a month, the entire staff will receive the points listed below:
   .5 points for each 1% over 100

7. Standard Performance: When the standard performance of the plant averages over 100% for a month, each individual in Shipping will receive points for each 1% above 100% as listed below:
   .25 points for each 1% over 100

Warehouse and Shipping Department reporting forms:
   • Housekeeping: Evaluations will be conducted on a weekly basis on unannounced days by 3 people (1 from general office, 2 from 100 Club Committee). Standard forms will be used and will be submitted weekly to the 100 Club Administrator.
   • Labor-hours per Truckload, Service C & A's, Inventory Adjustment, Overtime: The plant SAS will report these numbers to the 100 Club Administrator for calculation and recording.
   • Forklift inspection cards: The maintenance supervisor will review the cards and report who has reported 100% to the 100 Club Administrator.

E. Truck Drivers

1. Housekeeping: On a weekly basis, the unloading station will be evaluated. If the department earns an average of 2 points for the month, each individual will receive the listed points:
   1 point for every month

2. Loads Delivered: If a driver delivers an average of 12 loads a week for an entire month, that truck driver will receive the points listed below:
    2 points for every month

3. Miles Driven: If a driver has driven a percentage of miles equal to or greater than the percentage calculated by dividing the number of drivers into 100, (if there are four drivers then the driver must drive at least 25% of the total miles driven) he will receive the points listed below:
    1 point for every month

4. Bonus Miles Driven: If a driver drives an average of 1500 miles a week for an entire month, then the truck driver will receive the points listed below:
    1 point for every month

5. Accidents: If a truck driver goes for 9 months without receiving a traffic violation, not to include overweight tickets, he will receive the points listed below:
    10 points for 9 months

Truck driver reporting forms:
- Housekeeping: Evaluations will be conducted on a weekly basis on unannounced days by 3 people (1 from general office, 2 from 100 Club Committee). Standard forms will be used and will be submitted weekly to the 100 Club Administrator.
- Loads Delivered, Accidents, Traffic Violations: The SAS will forward to the 100 Club Administrator the daily shipment record and all accident and traffic violation reports for calculation and logging.

100 Club Housekeeping Inspection Guidelines for Major Manufacturing, Inc.

1. Inspections will be held in the last hour of the first shift or the first hour of the second shift. The day of the week must be a production day and be randomly drawn.

2. The inspection team is made up of one hourly 100 Club Committee member, one salary 100 Club Committee member and one person from the front office staff excluding the 100 Club Clerk. Which individuals are on the team will be decided by random draw. The team serves for one month before a new team is drawn.

3. The 100 Club Clerk will do the random drawing and inform the inspection team just prior to the inspection.

4. To get housekeeping points, a department must receive 75% of all available housekeeping inspection rating points.

5. Each inspector will tally points on individual inspection sheets; however, the final points for an inspection time will be the average of all three.

6. If an inspector is absent, the 100 Club Clerk will randomly pick a replacement from the area which the inspector represents.

7. Maximum points are shown on attached sheet, including the areas affected.

8. All inspection results will be posted weekly on the 100 Club bulletin board.

100 Club Inspection Team Weekly Report for Major Manufacturing, Inc.

Department	Value	Award	Comment
Guards			
Front lawn	1		
Areas near fence	1		
Guard shack	1		
Outside entry fence	1		
Front parking lot	1		
Front parking area / plant entrance	1		
Bushes trimmed and neat	1		
Back railroad gate area	1		
Total	**8**		
Quality Control			
Fife room	1		
Desk section	1		
Sink area	1		
Storage counter	1		
Scrubber area	1		
Upstairs storage	1		
Ovens and west counter	1		
South counter	1		
Inspection deck	1		
Fife monitors, console sink/swim solutions	1		
No shingles lying out in plant or parking lot	1		
Total	**11**		

Major Manufacturing Housekeeping Checklist

Department: GUARDS (Maximum Points: 8)

Objective	M	T	W	TH	F	S	S
Front lawn							
Areas near fence							
Guard shack							
Outside entry fence							
Front parking lot							
Front parking area/ plant entrance							
Bushes trimmed and neat							
Back railroad gate area							

Above are the areas of responsibility your department will be inspected on weekly. As the 100 Club Inspection Guidelines state, you must acquire 75% or better of your total possible points. This form is a recommended guide to help you establish your own intradepartment control.

U.S.A. COLLEGE

Perhaps no 100 Club installation was more surprising for me to learn about than the one at this small, mid-American college.

U.S.A. College was growing fast and losing its "sense of community," which troubled the provost. Today, because of the 100 Club, the college is enjoying not only a rekindling of the sense of community but a rekindling of the sense of "academic parsimony."

Department chairpersons as well as maintenance engineers wear 100 Club jackets to school. I've been told there are plans to expand the 100 Club to include the student body. I've often wished I could install a 100 Club in an elementary school district.

Logistically, a college is different from many other organizations. U.S.A. College has over one thousand employees, hundreds of offices, and scores of buildings spread over acres of rolling hills.

How did the 100 Club Administrator maintain up-to-date records of points and make him/herself available to answer questions? How did he/she track employee-generated suggestions, which was an important element of U.S.A. College's 100 Club objectives? Where were point tallies posted? Were report cards sent to the chairperson of the Education Department?

Evidently, with the fax machine, electronic mail, intra-campus mail delivery, and a huge bulletin board at the Student Union building, the ebb and flow of weekly, monthly, and quarterly reports to and from the 100 Club Administrator works like slick. I didn't ask if they send report cards to the chairperson of the Education Department.

100 Club Point Formula Chart for U.S.A. College
(based on an 8-month session)

Individual Category	Frequency	Points	Bonus	Total
Attendance	Monthly	4	10	42
Punctuality	Monthly	1		8
No discipline	Semester	5		10
No lost time injuries				
(On/off-the job)	Semester	5		10
Suggestions	As given	1/2		
Extra effort	As happens	5		
Longevity	9 Months	3+ Yrs.		3
In-college comms/				
Community Service	Semester	5		10
				83

DEPARTMENTS

Food Service

Creativity				
within budget	Monthly	2		16
Housekeeping	Monthly	2		16
Safety: No OSHA				
reportables	Semester	5		10
				42

Maintenance

Housekeeping	Monthly	2		16
Cooperation:				
inter & intra dept.	Monthly	2		16
Safety: No OSHA				
reportables	Semester	5		10
				42

Security

Physical fitness	Semester	5		10
Report accuracy	Monthly	2		16
Timely reports	Monthly	2		16
				42

Bookstore

Inventory control	Semester	5		10
Timely reports	Monthly	2		16
Money accuracy	Monthly	2		16
				42

Category	Frequency	Points	Bonus	Total
Health Center/Counseling				
Timely reports:				
student & college	Monthly	2		16
Timely claims				
handling	Monthly	2		16
Efficient scheduling	Monthly	1.5		12
				44
Admissions				
Timely responses	Monthly	2		16
Timely reports	Monthly	2		16
Inter/intra				
cooperation	Semester	5		10
				42
Data Processing				
Skill improvement	Monthly	2		16
Accuracy	Monthly	2		16
Inter/intra				
cooperation	Semester	5		10
				42
Audio/Visual Services				
Equipment maintenance	Monthly	1		8
Inter/intra cooperation	Semester	5		10
Accurate scheduling	Monthly	2		16
Skill upgrading	Semester	5		10
				44
Major Academic Departments				
(Includes dept. heads, professors, etc.)				
Timely course submission	Semester	5	5	15
Timely grade submission	Semester	5		10
Accuracy	Semester	5		10
Inter/intra dept.				
cooperation	Semester	5		10
				45
Collegewide				
Attendance	Semester	5		10
Voluntarism	College year	5		5
				15

SANDY'S FOOD DISTRIBUTION COMPANY

Sandy's is a regional food distribution company. It started out in a small warehouse, then moved to a larger warehouse, and now is located in a huge warehouse. It employs 55 people, including Sandy and his wife, Meg, who has run the back office for 34 years. It's hard to imagine a more Mom-and-Pop-type of operation than Sandy's Foods.

For the first 20 years, Sandy and Meg personally knew most of their workers, many of whom were second- and third-generation employees. But at some point in the company's growth, employee retention began to become a problem. Apparently the longevity of some employees created a hierarchy that discouraged the newer employees.

Sandy and Meg decided to install a 100 Club to help new employees feel a welcomed part of the older operation. Even though employee retention improved, so did overall performance.

100 Club Point Formula Chart for Sandy's Foods

Individual Categories

Individual recognition categories, listed below, are accompanied by a number of points. You will receive points as you fulfill the categories. These are the same things you've been doing in the past, but will now be recognized for. The Human Resources Department will record all points.

Hourly (Non-Exempt) Employees - Operations

Attendance	Perfect attendance for a period of one (1) month, earn 4 POINTS. 2 BONUS POINTS for a year of perfect attendance. Exceptions: Jury duty, death in the family, voluntary excused absence, and military duty.
Safety	3 POINTS will be given for a month free of work-related doctor-treated cases.
	2 BONUS POINTS will be given for a year of no doctor-treated cases.
Discipline	7 POINTS every 3 months for not receiving any written warnings for the 3-month period.
Community service	7 POINTS every year for participating in community service efforts. Examples: Donating blood, volunteer firefighter, being on a 100 Club subcommittee, coaching, working with Girl Scouts, Boy Scouts, church, school, civic services, etc. Just about anything! Each individual is responsible for letting us know so that points can be recorded.

Hourly (Non-Exempt) All Other Employees

Attendance	Perfect attendance for a period of one (1) month, earn 4 POINTS. 2 BONUS POINTS for a year of perfect attendance. Exceptions: Jury duty, death in the family, voluntary excused absence, and military duty.
No discipline	POINTS every 3 months for not receiving any written warnings for the 3-month period.

Community service   7 POINTS every year for participating in community service
                     efforts.
                        Examples: Donating blood, volunteer firefighter, being on a
                        100 Club subcommittee, coaching, working with Girl
                        Scouts, Boy Scouts, church, school, civic services, etc. Just
                        about anything! Each individual is responsible for letting us
                        know so that points can be recorded.

Accuracy of
    assignments   3 POINTS every month for 100% accuracy of all assignments.
                     2 BONUS POINTS for a year of 100% accuracy.

Timeliness of
    assignments   2 POINTS every month for timely completion of all
                     assignments.

Salaried (Exempt) Employees

Attendance   Perfect attendance for a period of one (1) month, earn 4
                     POINTS.
                     2 BONUS POINTS for a year of perfect attendance.

No discipline   1 POINT every 3 months for not receiving any written warnings
                     for the 3-month period.

Community service   7 POINTS every year for participating in community service
                     efforts.
                        Examples: Donating blood, volunteer firefighter, being on a
                        100 Club subcommittee, coaching, working with Girl
                        Scouts, Boy Scouts, church, school, civic services, etc. Just
                        about anything! Each individual is responsible for letting us
                        know so that points can be recorded.

Timeliness of
    assignments   3 POINTS every month for timely completion of all
                     assignments.
                     2 BONUS POINTS for a year of timely completion of all
                     assignments.

Departmental Categories

You will receive POINTS within your department for the following:

Warehouse (loaders & receivers, garage & maintenance)

Clean work areas	1 POINT per month for a clean assigned work area.
Forklift safety/ equipment	1 POINT per month for no damage to forklifts/ equipment
Accuracy	3 POINTS per month for 98-100% accuracy, timeliness, and completeness.

Transportation (drivers & routers)

Delivery	2 POINTS per month for no valid customer complaints against drivers each individual department.
Returned stops	1 POINT per month for no avoidable returned stops.
Safety	2 POINTS per month for no vehicle accidents.
Accuracy	2 POINTS per month for accuracy, timeliness, and completeness.

Trainers (driver/warehouse)

Timeliness & completeness	3 POINTS per month for timeliness and completeness of training
Training design program	2 POINTS for new and creative training methods.

Retail Store

Clean work area	2 POINTS per month for a clean work area.
Safety	2 POINTS per month for no lost time.
Customer complaints	1 POINT per month for no customer complaints.

Fish Room

Safety	3 POINTS per month for no lost time.
Clean work area	2 POINTS per month for a clean work area.

Outside Sales

Achieves sales goal	3 POINTS per month for achieving Sales goal.
Achieves gross profit dollars	3 POINTS per month for achieving gross profit dollars.
Achieves average lines per order goal	3 POINTS per month for achieving Average Lines per Order goal.

Achieves sales
   goal & gross
   profit dollars   6 BONUS POINTS per year.

Telemarketing/Customer Service
Timeliness &
   completeness   3 POINTS per month for the timeliness and completeness of
                 solving customer problems.

Achieving sales goal 3 POINTS per month for achieving specified sales goal.

Purchasing
Service level   3 POINTS per month for continuous periods of 98% or
                 better service level.

Buying opportunities 3 POINTS per month for seeking better buying opportunities.

Administration (accounting, clerical, driver-check-in, DP, personnel, AP & AR, cookie, customer pick-up, inventory, contracts)
Streamlining existing
   company procedures 2 POINTS per month for streamlining or simplifying existing
                 company procedures

Safety   1 POINT per month for no lost time.

Accuracy, timeliness   2 POINTS per month for accuracy, timeliness, and
                 completeness of all assignments.

Managers & Supervisors
Retention of
   employees   7 POINTS each year for the retention of 5 employees who
                 meet performance standards set by Sandy's Foods.

Training   2 POINTS per month for complete and effective training of
                 employees.

Accuracy, timeliness
   & completeness   3 POINTS per month for accuracy, timeliness, and com-
                 pleteness of all assignments.

Company Category
Cost-saving
suggestions   25 POINTS per year for a cost-saving suggestion that is
                accepted by management and implemented in the Company.

HOMETOWN FIRE DEPARTMENT

Of all the departments of municipal government, fire departments are the most naturally predisposed to the 100 Club. Thanking employees for doing a good job as assessed through a system of objective measurements is what the management culture of fire departments is all about.

First, the insurance industry through organizations like the Insurance Service Offices (IOS) has established a system of objectively measuring just about everything having to do with the quantitative and qualitative operations of a fire station. Second, the task-oriented, mission-driven interdependence and 24-hour camaraderie within a fire department make saying "Thank you" quite natural.

100 Club Point Formula Chart for Hometown Fire Department

Individual Category	Frequency	Points	Bonus	Total
Attendance	Monthly	3	10	37
Punctuality	Monthly	1	5	14
Safety/no lost time	9 months	15		15
No discipline	9 months	10		10
Physical fitness	9 months	15		15
Voluntarism	9 months	5		5
Suggestions	As given	1/2		—
				96
Department/Station				
Housekeeping/ interior & exterior	Monthly	2		18
Response to call-in departmentwide	Monthly	1		9
individual	Monthly	2		18
				45
Entire Department				
No lost time	3 months	5		15

REX'S RETAIL CLOTHING STORES, INC.

Rex's Retail Clothing Stores is a small chain operation with four sites, a central warehouse, and an administrative/buyer's office.

When I learned about Rex's 100 Club, I wrote and asked whether Rex's Retail Clothing Stores gives out 100 Club jackets, and if so what they looked like. From the description I was given over the phone, Rex's Retail Clothing Store's 100 Club jackets are much the same as Aardvark Appliance's 100 Club jackets. The cost to the company is about $13.

100 Club Point Formula Chart for Rex's Retail Clothing Stores, Inc.

Individual Category	Frequency	Points	Bonus	Total
Attendance	Monthly	4	10	46
Safety — no lost time	9 months	5		5
Response to call-ins	Monthly	2		18
Flexibility (cross-training)	9 months	5		5
Longevity	9 months	3+ # yrs.		3
Voluntarism	9 months	5		5
No discipline	9 months	10		10
Suggestions	As given	1/2		
Extra effort	As happens	5		—
				92

Departments

Buyers

Meet budgeted gross profit	Seasonally	5		20
Sales increases	Monthly	1	5	14
Timely markdowns	Monthly	1		9
				43

Stores

Sales goals	Monthly	2		18
Housekeeping	Monthly	1		9
Timely layaways/holds	Monthly	1		9
Scheduling accuracy	Monthly	1		9
				45

Warehouse

Timeliness & accuracy (individual job)	Monthly	1		9
Timeliness (total warehouse)	Monthly	2		18
Timely closing	Monthly	1		9
Housekeeping	Monthly	1		9
				45

Companywide

Reach sales forecast	Seasonally	2		8
Gross margin	Seasonally	2		8
				16

100 Club Point-Tracking Procedures and Definitions for Rex's Retail Clothing Stores, Inc.

Individual Categories

1. Attendance: A person who has 100% attendance for one month, excluding authorized absences such as leaves of absence, bereavement leave, vacations, shall receive 4 points. A person who has perfect attendance for a period of 9 consecutive months shall receive 10 bonus points.

2. Safety — no lost time: A person who stays injury-free for a period of 9 consecutive months shall receive 5 points.

3. Response to call-in: A person who reports into work when contacted by a supervisor — even though it is that person's day off — shall receive 2 points for each month of perfect response.

4. Flexibility (cross-training): A person who demonstrates flexibility by either volunteering to learn another job or by accepting a new assignment shall receive 5 points for each consecutive 9-month period.

5. Longevity: A person who remains in the employ of the company for 9 consecutive months shall receive 3 points for each 9-month period plus 1 additional point for each year of employment.

6. Voluntarism: A person who volunteers his/her time to community organizations (i.e., blood drive, youth sports team coaching, United Way, cancer drive, etc.) or business activities (i.e., picnic committee, safety committee, company newspaper, etc.) shall receive 5 points at the end of each 9-month period provided the activity is confirmed in writing on the letterhead of the respective organization.

7. No discipline: A person who has a perfect work record without instance of formal disciplinary action shall receive 10 points at the end of each 9 consecutive month period.

8. Suggestions: A person who submits suggestions to improve company efficiency or to promote a safer business environment shall receive 1 point for each bona fide suggestion, as determined by the 100 Club Oversight Committee, and 2 additional points if and when the idea is implemented.

9. Extra effort: A person determined by the 100 Club Oversight Committee to have demonstrated extra effort during the course of business shall receive 5 points for each instance of extra effort.

Department Categories

Buyers

1. Meet budgeted gross profit: All buyers shall receive 5 points at the end of each season in which the company meets its budgeted gross profit.

2. Sales increases: For each month there is a sales increase over the corresponding period in the preceding year, all buyers shall receive 1 point. If sales increases are recorded for 9 consecutive months, all buyers shall receive 5 bonus points.

3. Timely markdowns: All buyers shall receive 1 point for each month in which items are marked down in a timely manner in accordance with company markdown policy.

Stores

1. Sales goals: On a store-by-store basis, all employees shall receive 2 points for each month his/her store meets its sales goal.

2. Housekeeping: On a store-by-store basis, all employees shall receive 1 point for each month no demerits are issued for poor housekeeping practices.

3. Timely layaways/holds: On a store-by-store basis, all employees shall receive 1 point for each month all layaways and holds are handled in a timely fashion in accordance with posted company policy.

4. Scheduling accuracy: On a store-by-store basis, all employees shall receive 1 point for each month of accurate scheduling of employees.

Warehouse

1. Timeliness and accuracy of each individual job: Each individual employee shall receive 1 point for each month he/she performs his/her job in a timely and accurate manner.

2. Timeliness - total warehouse: All employees will receive 2 points for each month in which warehouse responsibilities are completed in a timely manner.

3. Timely closing: All employees shall receive 1 point for each month in which the month's closing is handled in a timely manner, in accordance with established company policy.

4. Housekeeping: All employees shall receive 1 point for each month no demerits are issued for poor housekeeping practices.

Company Categories

1. Reach sales forecast: All employees throughout the company shall receive 2 points for each season in which the company reaches its pre-determined sales forecast.

2. Gross margin: All employees throughout the company shall receive 2 points for each season in which the company achieves its gross margin.

Appendix A

A Comparison of Employee Suggestions in U.S., Japanese, and 100 Club Organizations

In recent studies by the Department of Labor, U.S. companies reported receiving 13 cost-saving suggestions per 100 employees with fewer than 25% of these suggestions actually being implemented. This compares with Japanese companies receiving 2,472 cost-saving suggestions per 100 employees, with 80% of these ideas actually being implemented.

In U.S. companies, only 8 employees out of 100 offer cost-saving suggestions, whereas in Japanese companies, 67 employees out of 100 offer cost-saving suggestions.

At companies that track the progress made by the 100 Club's suggestion system, here is what typically happens:

- 22 employees out of 100 routinely offer 168 cost-saving suggestions
- 54% of the suggestions are implemented.

Suggestion Plan Comparison
Per 100 Employees per Annum

	U.S.	JAPAN	100 CLUBS
No. of suggestions	13	2472	168
No. of employees submitting	8	67	22
No. of adoptions	3	1977	90
Adoption rate percentage	24%	80%	54%

Appendix B

Federal Mediation and Conciliation Service Impact Evaluation

Final Impact Evaluation of "The 100 Club"
Diamond International Corp.

A Labor-Management Cooperation Project
Partially Funded By
The Federal Mediation And Conciliation Service

November, 1983

Management Associates
88 Ridge Road
East Longmeadow, MA 01028

Thomas F. O'Connor, Ph.D.
J. Warren Goss

INDEX

FINAL REPORT

The following is a summary report of findings and conclusions drawn by Management Associates as a result of an impact evaluation of "The 100 Club" Program as first instituted at Diamond International Corporation, Palmer, Massachusetts.

"The 100 Club" is the program design as conceptualized at Diamond International. The Federal Mediation and Conciliation Service, through its Labor-Management Cooperation Program, provided partial funding to use the Palmer Plant as the model for the expansion of "The 100 Club" into three other plants in Diamond's Fiber Products Division — Natchez, Mississippi; Red Bluff, California; and Plattsburgh, New York. All four plants have, as the collective bargaining agent for unionized employees, Locals of the United Paperworkers International Union.

The major objective of the Program simply stated is to recognize employees for positive, all-encompassing work-related efforts. This has resulted in increased industrial productivity through enhanced Labor-Management relations.

Diamond International is a multi-state, multi-plant operation which produces a variety of products. In terms of Labor-Management relations, productivity, absenteeism, accidents, grievances and quality control, it was, perhaps, no better nor worse than most product-oriented businesses Late in 1980, Diamond International authorized the creation of "The 100 Club" with first emphasis on improving attendance and reducing accidents.

In February 1980, "The 100 Club" was launched in the Palmer Plant, followed by staggered starting dates at the other plants; August 1981 — Natchez; April 1982 — Red Bluff; August 1982 — Plattsburgh. Project Director was Daniel C. Boyle, Palmer Personnel Manager and author of "The 100 Club." Its purpose had been expanded to include nearly every aspect of the work environment; foremost among these was plant-wide productivity. A reward system was introduced. The rewards were "points" which could be earned for performing certain functions or at certain levels. The acquisition of 100 points functions made one a member of "The 100 Club" and earned the individual a jacket. Tallies of more points led to additional gifts.

The gifts earned with points are not particularly expensive and well within the workers' purchasing power if they wanted to buy them on the market. The basic premise, then, of "The 100 Club" was not "buy" increased profits and productivity with gifts but to demonstrate Management's interest in and concern for its employees, which would bring about a corresponding interest and concern of employees for their jobs and productivity. Initial data demonstrates "The 100 Club" to be an overwhelming success.

The methodology used to evaluate "The 100 Club" employed two sets of data; one, hard data concerning absenteeism, grievances recorded, productivity, accidents, quality control and disciplinary actions and, two, soft data — attitudes of employees towards their work and the Company.

The hard data was supplied by Company records; the soft data by questionnaires filled out anonymously by both Labor and Management personnel. Complete data for all four Diamond International Plants (Palmer, Ma.; Natchez, Miss.; Red Bluff, Ca.; and Plattsburgh, N.Y.) has now been completed. The information from Palmer, Ma. Plant is the most complete but the information from the other plants is, so far, corresponding to the Palmer findings.

Without compromising the Company's confidential information, we can state that gross financial benefits generated by the Palmer Plant have, since the introduction of "The 100 Club," increased by over $1,600,000. This increase came about by a dramatic increase in productivity caused, in part, by a 42% decrease in absenteeism, a 40% decrease in quality-related mistakes, a 72% decrease in grievances filed, a 48% decrease in disciplinary actions, and a 43.7% drop in lost-time caused by accidents with a corresponding drop of over $35,000 in Workmen's Compensation costs.

It must be stressed that one major aspect in the success of "The 100 Club" is the relationship between Labor and Management. The Program was implemented jointly and a combined Labor-Management Committee, with employee volunteers, oversees program changes. In addition to discussions on allocations of points, the Committee meets regularly to deal with problems impacting on employees. Also, it is not unusual for members of Management to share product cost-related data at these sessions.

"How else can we expect employees to become familiar with the plights we face unless we share crucial operations-oriented information with them," asks Program Developer Daniel C. Boyle, describing employee involvement at the Palmer Plant. "Once employees are aware of our problems — and believe we are leveling with them — they unite to become our 'partners for progress'."

Thus, the overall success of "The 100 Club" has as its core the improved relationship between Labor and Management since the institution of the employee recognition program with its concomitant positive improvement in Company productivity and profit, neither of which were envisioned nor planned for at the inception of the program.

This opinion is based on comparisons of employee attitudes existing in the Palmer Plant during the summer of 1980, when a preliminary survey was taken, and similar surveys administered during 1983. It must be noted that the initial survey was designed to gauge potential employee involvement in plant-wide activities and not specifically linked to what was to become known as "The 100 Club."

BASE LINE ATTITUDINAL SURVEY

The base line attitudinal survey administered by the Company in 1980, in additional to their questions, addressed three (3) fundamental issues which required responses from Labor employees concerning their perception of the following:

1. Whether or not they were treated with "respect" by Management.

2. Whether they approached their work tasks with a "pessimistic" or optimistic" attitude.

3. Whether or not they were "rewarded" for a job well done.

RESPONSE from the sample population selected indicate:

1. 65% felt *that they were not treated respectfully* by *Management.*
   27% felt that *they were usually treated respectfully.*
   13% felt that *they were sometimes treated respectfully.*

2. 44% approached their work with *optimism.*
   56% approached their work with *pessimism.*

3. 79% felt that *they were not rewarded for a job well done.*
   21% felt that *they were rewarded for a job well done.*

"POST" ATTITUDINAL SURVEY

The "post" attitudinal survey, when compared with the responses elicited in the "base line," as shown above, reveal the following:

1. 86% of the Labor employees feel that the Company and Management feel that *they are "very important" or "important."*

2. 81% responded that work provided them with *"recognition by the Company"* and 73% said that the Company showed *"concern for them as people."*

    On the average, 79% said their attitude toward the quality of their work and product was "of much greater concern" to them.

3. 77% felt that they were being rewarded for a job well done through *"recognition," "self-satisfaction,"* and concern by the Company for them *"as persons."*

The post survey results, as reflected above, indicate a very significant, positive shift in Labor's attitude toward themselves, the quality of their work environment and their perceptions of Management.

It is the evaluators' opinion that this significant shift toward positive attitudes and the concomitant closer inter-personal relationships between Management and Labor is a key indicator to be used in assessing the etiology of the hard performance data.

As previously noted, the base line data was available only for the Palmer Plant. Once Corporate Management saw the successes of "The 100 Club" in the first plant, they directed expansions into other facilities.

In spite of the absence of base line data, "post" attitudinal surveys administered at the Diamond plants in Natchez, Red Bluff and Plattsburgh show employee attitudes at these plants to be reasonably compatible with those present in Palmer.

As mentioned, the attitudinal surveys concerning the quality of work life support the conclusions drawn from the hard data which follows. The hard data consists of key measurable factors using 1980 as the base year, the year prior to the introduction of "The 100 Club" at the Palmer Plant.

The following are narratives relevant to the key measures.

The evaluators' opinion is based on hard data relating to seven key measures, of a quantified nature, reported from the four Diamond plants involved in the program.

It should be noted that there are dissimilarities of a significant nature in each of the participating plants which should be taken into account when reviewing the data which follows; e.g. The Palmer Plant, in operation since 1934 and employing 325 persons, was the "genesis" location. Data collection and procedures for same were more closely controlled and standardized. Data gaps identified in Palmer, of necessity, would require Palmer as the "control" plant to transmit such gap information to the other plants with recommendations for change in the collection system. These changes were not always implemented exactly as requested by Palmer, hence reporting was not in all cases exactly the same as the Palmer Plant. As a consequence, exact comparisons, inter-plant, were not always available to the evaluators. Where major inconsistencies have been detected, they have been so noted in this report and taken into account in reporting results.

1. The Natchez Plant, the newest of the four plants, was opened in February 1965. There, over 300 persons were

employed. During the reporting period, 1981-1983, little, if any, machine or equipment upgrading was taking place.

2. The Red Bluff Plant was constructed in the mid-1950's. It, also, had approximately 300 employees. Progressionally, it was the third Diamond Plant to implement "The 100 Club." There was little capital expenditure during the reporting period.

3. Plattsburgh, New York, vintage 1935 and with 250 employees, participated in the program only for one year since it was the last to become involved in "The 100 Club."

All of the aforementioned anomalies in both time in the program and data collection variations notwithstanding, the evaluators found a consistency of results which clearly support the conclusion drawn in the preliminary report of June, 1983. These results, by key measure, are as follows:

1. PRODUCTIVITY INCREASE

All four plants report a significant productivity increase since the introduction of "The 100 Club" into the individual plant. The average increase in productivity for all four plants for the entire period covered is 14.5%, a figure that might be misleadingly low.

A trend in both the Palmer and Natchez plants indicates that the longer "The 100 Club" has been in operation, the greater the productivity increase has been. For example, Palmer's increase in its first year was 12% over base line; its second year was 14% over base line.

Natchez shows an increase of 4.5% the first year, 1981 ("The 100 Club" operated only 4 months of 1981); 7.5 in the second year, 1982; and 19% the third year, 1983.

The Red Bluff and Plattsburgh data indicate less than a full year of complete information. If the trend continues for the latter two plants, as it did for the former two, the average increase would be higher. Also, Red Bluff and Plattsburgh are older plants, thus making increased productivity more difficult without significant capital expenditures as machines have more historic down-time than in newer plants.

Some plants (noted below) reported productivity based on certain machines as those machines were the only ones whose productivity could be consistently measured or that productivity increase differed by machine within a given plant. Nevertheless, a 14.5% average increase in productivity is significant in itself.

Again, without compromising confidential information, we can state that gross financial benefits generated by "The 100 Club" via the 14.5% average productivity increase is over $5,200,000.

Individual plant data on productivity increases follows; N = output.

Palmer

1980-1981*	N =	1,357,000
1981-1982	N =	1,532,000
1982-1983	N =	1,581,000
Total Increase	N =	224,000

% Increase = 16.5%

---

*Palmer's productivity data based on "The 100 Club" year, not calendar year.

<u>Natchez</u> (Data is for #1 machine only because of its consistency of volume.)

1980	N =	1,051,909
1981	N =	1,088,181
1982	N =	1,136,545
1983	N =	1,293,727

Total Increase   N =   241,818

% Increase = 19%

Red Bluff
<u>Duplex Poly Wrap Machine</u>

1982	N =	350,000,000
1983	N =	413,000,000

Total Increase   N =   63,000,000

% Increase = 18%

<u>RB-3 Machine</u>

1982	N =	427,000,000
1983	N =	456,000,000

Total Increase   N =   27,000,000

% Increase = 7%

<u>Plattsburgh</u>

1982	N =	1,351,000 (daily average)
1983	N =	1,494,000 (daily average)

Total Increase   N =   143,000

% Increase = 10%

2. QUALITY RELATED ERRORS

Plants reported customer complaints concerning quality of products in the aggregate for the time period being reported.

Thus, it is not possible to refine the figures any further than they are. Three plants reported on quality related errors. The fourth did not because many of the produced products were still in shipment and data was not available. However, the figures for the other three plants speak for themselves.

Palmer
1981-1983 — quality-related errors reduced by 40%.

Natchez
1981-1983 — quality-related errors reduced by 53%.

Red Bluff
1982-1983 — no appreciable reduction in quality-related errors; however, production increased by 18% on one machine and 7% on another with no loss of quality.

Plattsburgh
1983 — information not available since reporting period ended on 10/1/83 and errors information will not be received timely enough to include in this study.

3. ABSENTEEISM

A key element of "The 100 Club" is to reward people for attendance. Three of the four plants report a dramatic reduction in absenteeism since the introduction of "The 100 Club" into the plant. The fourth, Red Bluff, showed so significant change in attendance.

N is the number of person days of absenteeism per year. Average reduction of absenteeism is 32%.

Palmer

1980-1981	N = 3,303
1981-1982	N = 2,410
1982-1983	N = 1,882
1983-1984	N = 1,805 (projected)

Total Decrease   N = 1,421

% Decrease = 48%

Natchez

1981-1983 — Natchez reports a 48% reduction in absenteeism.

Red Bluff

1982-1983 — No appreciable change reported.

Plattsburgh

| 1982 | N = 2,863 |
| 1983 | N = 1,743 (up to period ending August, 1983) |

Total Decrease   N = 1,121

% Decrease = 39%

4. GRIEVANCES

The reduction in employee initiated grievances is reflected by a high (-72%) at Palmer, -52% at Plattsburgh, -47% at Natchez with Red Bluff not reporting. A three plant simple average equals -57%.

Correspondingly, disciplinary actions instituted by the Company are down a simple average of 44% in the plants reporting (Palmer and Plattsburgh).

<u>Palmer</u>
1980-1981	N = 150
1981-1982	N = 50
1982-1873	N = 43

Disciplinary actions down 48% since introduction of "The 100 Club."

<u>Red Bluff</u>
Information not included.

<u>Plattsburgh</u>
1981	N = 25
1982	N = 13 — 48% decline
1983	N = 6 — 54% decline

5. INDUSTRIAL ACCIDENTS

Three of the four plants reported on the decrease in industrial accidents; Red Bluff did not report and Natchez reported percentages, not actual numbers.

The reduction in industrial accidents brings obvious savings in Workmen's Compensation claims and overtime costs, as well as increased morale and sense of safety amongst the workers.

N equals the number of days lost per year due to accidents (% Decrease = 48.6%). The average reduction in industrial accident days is 41%.

Palmer
1980-1981	N =	711
1981-1982	N =	518
1982-1983	N =	401
1983-1984	N =	365 (projected)

Total Decrease N = 3346

Natchez

Natchez reports a 48% decrease in number of days lost to industrial accidents from 1981-1983 and a 28% decrease in number of accidents.

Plattsburgh
| 1982 | N = | 689 |
| 1983 | N = | 478 |

Total Decrease N = 211

Total Decrease in Days Lost = 31%

6. NON-SCHEDULED MACHINE DOWN-TIME

Diamond International divides its year into thirteen reporting periods and also includes in its budget money for non-scheduled machine down-time. Thus, the data reported below is in terms of reported periods being above or below budgeted figures. When below, the machine is in production for longer periods. When above budget, the machine is out of production.

<u>Palmer</u>

1980	Above budget 11 of 13 periods
1981-1982	Below 11 of 13 periods for 22% savings
1982-1983	Below budget 10 of 13 periods, at or within acceptable deviation from standard for 26% savings

<u>Natchez</u>
No information available at this time.

<u>Plattsburgh</u>

1982	Below budget 10 of 13 periods
1983	Below budget 4 of 8 periods

7. DECREASE IN OVERTIME COSTS

This factor is one of high complexity since a decrease in over-time can be caused by any of a number of factors, e.g. a marked reduction in sales and inventory on hand, a cost controlling decision by management unrelated to inventory, etc. It is the evaluators' opinion, however, that the dramatic decrease in lost-time accidents, increased attendance and decreased unauthorized absences is the most probable cause of the significant reduction in overtime. Company management confirms that the sales/inventory/conscious decision factors are not relevant.

<u>Palmer</u>
"Significant" decrease; especially noted in Shipping.

<u>Natchez</u>
8/81-7/83 reduced by 18% compared to the two preceding years.

Red Bluff
No information.

Plattsburgh
Hard to measure - machines operating five days during reporting period instead of six days as was the case in previous period.

MANAGEMENT AND ADMINISTRATION OF "THE 100 CLUB"

Of concern to the evaluators was Management's perception of the level of difficulty involved in administering "The 100 Club." Explicit in the operation of the program was the need to collect data, maintain records and attend meetings related to the program.

The chart reflects the aggregate responses of Managers in each of the four plants to the questions posed in the "Management" survey. (See page 121 for sample of questionnaire.)

Plant	Complexity	Management Time
Palmer	Relatively simple	Less than 15%
Natchez	Relatively simple	20%*
Red Bluff	Relatively simple	Less than 15%
Plattsburgh	Relatively simple	Less than 15%

Plant	Staff Time	Added Responsibility
Palmer	Less than 15%	Acceptable addition
Natchez	5%*	Minor addition
Red Bluff	Less than 15%	Minor addition
Plattsburgh	Less than 15%	Minor addition

* Exact count of time was recorded by this plant.

Management, Labor, and Administration of 100 Club
(Sample Questionnaire)

I find the general administration of the 100 Club and its activities to be:

Relatively simple	( )
Of moderate complexity	( )
Difficult but manageable	( )
Too complex	( )

I find the time devoted by myself to the administration of the 100 Club to be:

1% - 15%	( )
16% - 25%	( )
26% - 50%	( )
51% - 100%	( )

I find the time devoted by my staff to administering the 100 club to be:

1% - 15%	( )
16% - 25%	( )
26% - 50%	( )
51% - 100%	( )

I find the additional responsibility of administering the 100 Club to be:

No problem	( )
A minor addition of work	( )
An acceptable addition to my workload	( )
A major problem to my workload	( )

CONCLUSIONS

1. "The 100 Club" program design as conceptualized and implemented, upon analysis of available data, can assuredly be deemed an outstanding success after viewing both the preliminary and final data.

2. One might fairly ask whether or not other variables might have produced the positive changes in those key indicators and measures which are reported on herein and attributed to "The 100 Club" program.

    It is the evaluators' opinion that, absent hard data of a comparably positive character, clearly ascribable to one or more of the other possible variables and which are demonstrated as being present in the same or similar industry, the operative element effecting the changes reported on are fairly attributable to "The 100 Club."

    It should be noted that no data from other industries reflecting changes comparable to those at Diamond International have come to the evaluators' attention.

3. The evaluators' conclusion, drawn from attitudinal measures derived from the tailored instruments when coupled with the hard data reported earlier on, is that the "quality of work life" for Company employees, both Management and Labor, has improved in direct relation to the remarkable changes demonstrated by the quantified data which speaks so positively for itself.

Attachment A
Summary of Key Indicator Changes
Percentage of Productivity

	Pre 100 Club	Most Current	No. Change	% Change
Palmer	1,357,000	1,581,000	+224,000[1]	+16.5%
Natchez	1,051,909	1,293,727	+241,818[1]	+19.0%
Red Bluff	A) 350,000,000	A) 413,000,000	A) +63,000,000[2]	A)+18.0%
	B) 427,000,000	B) 456,000,000	B) +27,000,000[2]	B)+10.0%
Plattsburgh	1,351,000	1,494,000	+143,000[1]	+10.0%

Summary of Key Indicator Changes
% Change During Report Period

Grievances

Palmer	72% reduction in grievances
Natchez	47% reduction in grievances
Red Bluff	N/A
Plattsburgh	52% reduction in grievances

Instances of Disciplinary Action

Palmer	48% decline
Plattsburgh	40% decline

Absenteeism

Palmer	48% decline
Natchez	48% decline
Red Bluff	No change
Plattsburgh	39% decline

Lost Time Due to Industrial Accidents

Palmer	48.6% decrease
Natchez	48.0% decrease
Plattsburgh	31.0% decrease

---

[1] Daily production average
[2] Yearly production average

Attachment B

TO: ALL EMPLOYEES PARTICIPATING IN THIS SURVEY

FROM: EVALUATION CONTRACTOR

As an independent evaluation contractor designated by your Company and the Federal Mediation and Conciliation Service (United States Department of Labor), we are undertaking the examination of Labor-Management relations and industrial productivity. We have prepared the questionnaire which you are being given today to aid us in our evaluation.

You have been designated BY COMPUTER SELECTION to participate in this study and your participation is appreciated.

THE SURVEY IS DESIGNED TO INSURE CONFIDENTIALITY. The Evaluation Team will know you only as a number and the results of the survey will in no way identify you as a person.

Your response should be placed in the envelope provided, SEALED and returned to the Coordinator, who will assure that they are mailed directly to the Evaluation Team.

NO ONE IN YOUR COMPANY WILL SEE THESE RESPONSES.

Please be completely honest in your responses.

Thank you.

Appendix C

Glossary of 100 Club Terms

activity: A work habit selected for recognition, such as "attendance." It must be measurable, preferably from an objective standpoint.

100 Club administrator: The person who performs the record-keeping function, attends all committee meetings and is responsible for keeping management and employees up-to-date on changes in the club's mechanics.

bonus points: Points which are issued to employees whose work record shows continuous effort over an extended period of time. (For example, 9 months of perfect attendance may result in 10 bonus points.)

CEO: The top ranking administrator within an organization, such as Chief Executive Officer, President, Plant Manager, Hospital Administrator, Mayor, City Manager, Principal, etc.

department subcommittee: A group of employees acting as a line of communication between the department's employees and the Oversight Committee. Preferably, each subcommittee is limited to five (5) members. One (1) member is designated to serve on the oversight committee each month.

design committee: Consists of representatives of management and the employees who are responsible for tailoring the 100 Club to meet the needs of the organization.

facilitator: The management person designated to gather and sort through information generated in the design sessions. Also, responsible for keeping the design committee members focused on the mission at hand.

frequency: That point in time (i.e., day, week, month, quarter, year) at which points will be given.

highly rated activities: As activities for which employees will receive recognition/points are identified, they are ranked according to which will generate the highest to lowest number of points. By design, individual activities are highly rated.

oversight committee: Consists of equal numbers of management representatives and employee representatives and is responsible for answering questions and settling disputes in connection with all aspects of the 100 Club. Must meet on a monthly basis.

point formula: In order for 30% of the employees to be able to reach the 100-point level by the end of the ninth month, the total point availability must be between 140 and 160. This is divided as follows: Individual Effort: 84 to 96 points; Department/Team Effort: 42 to 48 points; Organizationwide/Plantwide Effort: 14 to 16 points.

point formula chart: During the design session, the facilitator gathers information from committee members and records this data on a large piece of paper with the following headings: Activity, Frequency, Number of Points, Bonus Points, Total Points.

report card: A line item by line item breakdown of points received by employees for each activity. This report, personally signed by a key management representative, is sent to each employee's home.

10-week timetable: Once the management design session is completed, it takes 10 weeks before the 100 Club gets underway. During this time period, management re-creates the design process with employee representatives.

Appendix D

100 Club Bibliography

The Journal Register, Palmer, MA – June 2, 1983
"Diamond Productivity Cited at Thorndike Plant"

The Washington Times, Washington, DC – June 3, 1983
"Incentives Boost Job Production"

The Daily News, Springfield, MA – June 3, 1983
"Productivity Program Enhances Divested Plant"

Daily Labor Report, Washington, DC – June 6, 1983
"Federal Aid to Labor-Management Panels Justified by Results, Participants Say"

Transcript-Telegram, Holyoke, MA – June 30, 1983

The Daily News, Springfield, MA – July 1, 1983
"Palmer Workers Score 100 in TIME Magazine Article"

TIME – July 4, 1983
"Hot 100: A Million-Dollar Incentive Plan."

Industry Week – July 25, 1983
"A Diamond of a Productivity Idea."

Enterprise, David, CA – July 27, 1983
Column by Bob Dunning

White House Conference on Productivity, Washington, DC – July 1983
news clips

BNA Bulletin to Management – August 11, 1983

Pulp & Paper Week – August 22-26, 1983
"'100 Club' Boosts Productivity"

Pulp And Paper – October 1983
"'100 Club' Boosts Mill Productivity"

Incentive Marketing – October 1983
"Worker Woes? Motivate the Good Ones, Not the Bad"

The Levinson Letter – December 15, 1983
The Levinson Institute, Inc., Cambridge, MA
"MANAGEMENT – Tokens of Appreciation"

Federal Mediation And Conciliation Service, Office of Information,
Washington, DC – February 6, 1984
"Government Study Verifies Productivity Increases through Employee
Recognition"

Productivity Improvement Bulletin, Waterford, CT – February 25, 1984
"Build Employee Commitment to Productivity Growth"

Aerosol Age – May 1984
"Heekin Can Offers Employee Incentive Program"

Owens-Corning Fiberglas Information Newsletter,
Toledo, OH – January 1985
"RRD Recognition Program Makes First Awards"

The Brookville Democrat, Brookville, IN – March 20, 1985
"New Program at Owens/Corning to Recognize and Reward Employees"

Nation's Business – May 1985
"Who's in Charge Here?"

The 100 Club Reports, Holyoke, MA – Summer 1985

National Productivity Report, Wheaton, IL – July 31, 1985
"The 100 Club Spreads from Coast to Coast"

Industry – August 1985
"Focus on Change"

Cincinnati Post Neighbors, Cincinnati, OH – June 24, 1986
"Bonus Rewards Job Well Done at Heekin Can"

Owens-Corning Fiberglas Information Newsletter,
Toledo, OH – June/July 1986
"Four RRD Plants Celebrate 100 Club Anniversary"

Small Business Report – October 1986
"Case History: Employee Recognition Programs"

PIMA – October 1986
"Effective Management: Want to Amaze Your Employees? Tell Them You
Like Their Work"

The Myths & Methods of Being a Manager by Kandy Kidd, "Are Rewards
Merely a Penny for Your Thoughts?"
Brendon Hill Publishing, Oakland, CA, October, 1986

The Valley News, Fulton, NY – December 18, 1986
"Nestle '100 Club'"

Plant Services – February 1987
"The 100 Club: A Shining Example of Successful Labor/Management
Relations"

Harvard Business Review – March-April 1987
"Ideas for Action: The 100 Club"

Creative Management – April 1987
"Psychic Income: The 80/20 Rule for Managers"

CUE/Clearinghouse, CUE/NAM, Washington, DC – April 15, 1987
"Employees Proud to Join 100 Club; It Recognizes Their Value to
Company"

Food Store Magazine – April/May 1987
"People: An Employee Recognition Plan that Works!"

Boxboard Containers – May 1987
"Viewpoint: Employee Involvement Recognition Can Save $$"

Personnel Management Alert Newsletter – June 1987
Management Resource Association
Institute of Management, Milwaukee, WI

The Pryor Report – June 1987
"Productivity Incentive – The 100 Club"

The Informed Executive – June 15, 1987
Newsletter of Employers Resource Council, Cleveland, OH

Manufacturer & Employer Association – June 24, 1987
News & Views – Circular Letter No. Y-29
"The '100 Club' – Recognizes Good Workers – Yields Amazing Results"

The Christian Science Monitor – June 25, 1987
"Softer Voices at Bargaining Tables? Hard Times Spawn Innovations in
Labor-Management Relations"

Briefs, Greater Cincinnati Employers Institute – June 26, 1987
"Productivity Incentive"

Paper, Film & Foil Converter – June 1987
"Profit Probe: Employee Involvement Stressed in Recognition Program"

Paper, Film & Foil Converter – July 1987
"Profit Probe: Employee Involvement Program Creates Positive
Environment"

Central Illinois Employers' Association Facts Bulletin 7 – July 1, 1987
"'100 Club' Increases Productivity"

American Association Of Industrial Management – July 1987
"The Name of the Game Is Productivity"

The Rotarian – September 1987
"In Management, It's Surprising What a Simple 'Thank You' Can Do"

FMI Digest – October 1987
Food Marketing Institute, Washington, DC
"Employee Club Boosts Morale, Attendance, Efficiency"

The Patriot, Fulton, NY – October 20, 1987
"Nestle Promotes '100 Club'"

The Valley News, Fulton, NY – October 20, 1987
"Nestle Welcomes Employees into '100 Club'"

Incentive Marketing – December 1987
"Employee Motivation: Recognition That Works"

America Works – 1988
The Report of the President's Advisory Committee on Mediation and
Conciliation, Washington, DC

Nation's Business – March 1988
"Motivating For Success — 2. Recognize Your Employees"

Healthy Companies – Summer 1988
"Recognition: The Winning Strategy"

ProMat News, Johannesburg, S.A. – August 1988
"This Is What Motivation Is All About" — "Now Let's Try Human
Relations"

The Jerry Williams Show – March 14, 1989
WRKO Radio, Boston, MA
Talk Show on Employee Appreciation

The Union Leader, Manchester, NH – March 20, 1989
"Small Gifts for Good Work Can Make a Big Difference"

The Wall Street Journal – May 2, 1989
Labor Letter – "We Love You"

The Boston Globe, Boston, MA – July 4, 1989
"Seeking an Edge: Incentives Prove Their Worth"

The Arizona Republic, Phoenix, AZ – July 16, 1989
"'100 Club' Offers Workers Incentive"

Management, by John A. Pearce II and Richard B. Robinson, Jr.
Random House Business Division, New York, 1989.
Chapter 13 – "Human Resource Management and Labor Relations:
Employee Recognition Programs at Diamond Fiber Products"

Competitiveness: The Executive's Guide to Succe$$, by L. William Seidman
and Steven L. Skancke, M.E. Sharpe, Armonk, NY, 1989.

Spirit of Consol, by Anthony Hooking, Hollards South Africa, Bethulie,
Republic of South Africa, 1989

*The Loyalty Factor – A Management Guide to the Changing Dynamics of
Loyalty in the Workplace,* by Carol Kinsey Goman, Ph.D., KCS Publishing,
Berkeley, CA – 1990.
Chapter 4 – "A Culture for Loyalty: Recognition Programs"

The Daily News, Durban, S.A. – October 18, 1990
"Clubbing Together to Improve Worker Productivity"

The Sunday Tribune, Durban, S.A. – October 28, 1990
"Club Boosts Employee Morale"

The Loyalty Factor – Building Trust in Today's Workplace, by Carol Kinsey Goman, Ph.D., MASTERMEDIA Limited, New York – 1991.
Chapter 4 – "A Culture for Loyalty: Recognition Programs"

Investor's Daily – CEO Briefing: "These Lovely Gifts"

HR Magazine – October 1992
Society for HR Management
"Employee Motivation that Works"

Supervision – November 1992
National Research Bureau, Burlington, IA
"To Employees – 'Thanks' Means Millions — Literally"

Manufacturing Systems – February 1994
"Employees as 'Point Persons'"

Total Employee Involvement Newsletter – April 1994
TEI Institute, Productivity, Inc., Norwalk, CT
"The 100 Club: A Time-Tested Recognition Plan"

Total Productive Maintenance Newsletter – April 1994
American Institute for Total Productive Maintenance,
Productivity, Inc., Norwalk, CT
"Saying Thanks — The 100 Club: An Ideal Way to Recognize TPM Achievements"

BNA Bulletin to Management – July 14, 1994
"Policy Guide — Recognition Raises Productivity"

Total Employment Involvement, 13th National Conference –
October 27-28, 1994
"Enlist Your Workforce in the Re-engineering Revolution"
(paper by the author)

About the Author

Daniel C. Boyle is an internationally known lecturer, writer and consultant on Employee Recognition, Motivation, Team Building and Communication. A former newspaper reporter, editor, and columnist, he received a B.A. in Political Science from the Colorado College. He and his wife, Angela, live in South Hadley, Mass., where he is currently at work on a second book.

Other Books from Productivity Press

Productivity Press provides individuals and companies with materials they need to achieve excellence in quality, productivity and the creative involvement of all employees. Through sets of learning tools and techniques, Productivity supports continuous improvement as a vision, and as a strategy. Many of our leading-edge products are direct source materials translated into English for the first time from industrial leaders around the world.

Call toll-free 1-800-394-6868 for our free catalog.

The Improvement Engine
Creativity and Innovation through Employee Involvement
The Kaizen Teian System
JHRA (ed.)

The Improvement Engine offers the most all inclusive information available today on this proven method for increasing employee involvement. Kaizen Teian is a technique developed in Japan for encouraging employees to constantly look for and make improvement suggestions. This book explores the subtitles between designing a moderately successful program and a highly successful one and includes with a host of tools, techniques and case studies.
ISBN 1-56327-010-2 / 155 pages / $40.00 / Order IMPENG-B248

Motivating Superior Performance
Saul W. Gellerman

Money is seldom the most effective motivator. It's expensive and to get the most effective results you have to know how to use it wisely. If money doesn't work, what does? Saul Gellerman offers you specific guidelines on what does and doesn't motivate. From looking at motivating individuals, groups, to how stress affects motivation down to when money is a major motivator (when hiring a new employee), *Motivating Superior Performance* shows you how to get more from your employees and yourself.
ISBN 1-56327-063-3 / 47 pages / $15.95 / Order MS5-B248

Productivity Press, Inc. Dept. BK, P.O. Box 13390, Portland, OR 97213-0390
Telephone: 1-800-394-6868 Fax: 1-800-394-6286

Doing and Rewarding
Inside a High-Performance Organization
Carl G. Thor

The high-performance organization has certain special characteristics, habits, and systems. Its focus is on satisfying the customer; the leadership is active, involved and competitive; the employees are informed and knowledgeable, and there is a strong reward system in place. Programs such as gainsharing plans help to recognize and reward performance results. In *Doing and Rewarding: Inside a High-Performance Organization,* you'll learn how to design a reward system that supports your goals.
ISBN 1-56327-061-7 / 56 pages / $15.95 / Order MS6-B248

Caught in the Middle
A Leadership Guide for Partnership in the Workplace
Rick Maurer

Managers today are caught between old skills and new expectations. You're expected not only to improve quality and services, but also to get staff more involved. This stimulating book provides the inspiration and know-how to achieve these goals as it brings to light the rewards of establishing a real partnership with your staff. Includes self-assessment questionnaires.
ISBN 1-56327-004-8 / 258 pages / $30.00 / Order CAUGHT-B248

CEDAC
A Tool for Continuous Systematic Improvement
Ryuji Fukuda

CEDAC encompasses three tools for continuous systematic improvement: window analysis (for identifying problems), the CEDAC diagram (a modification of the classic "fishbone diagram," for analyzing problems and developing standards), and window development (for ensuring adherence to standards). This manual provides directions for setting up and using CEDAC. Sample forms included.
ISBN 0-915299-26-7 / 144 pages / $55.00 / Order CEDAC-B248

Productivity Press, Inc. Dept. BK, P.O. Box 13390, Portland, OR 97213-0390
Telephone: 1-800-394-6868   Fax: 1-800-394-6286

Feedback Toolkit
16 Tools for Better Communication in the Workplace
Rick Maurer

In companies striving to reduce hierarchy and foster trust and responsible participation, good person-to-person feedback can be as important as sophisticated computer technology in enabling effective teamwork. Feedback is an important map of your situation, a way to tell whether you are "on or off track." Used well, feedback can motivate people to their highest level of performance. Despite its significance, this level of information sharing makes most managers uncomfortable. *Feedback Toolkit* addresses this natural hesitation with an easy-to-grasp 6-step framework and 16 practical and creative approaches for giving and receiving feedback with individuals and groups. Maurer's reality-tested methods in *Feedback Toolkit* are indispensable equipment for managers and teams in every organization.
ISBN 1-56327-056-0 / 109 pages / $15.00 / Order FEED-B248

The Teamwork Advantage
An Inside Look at Japanese Product and Technology Development
Jeffrey L. Funk

How are so many Japanese manufacturing firms shortening product time-to-market, reducing costs, and improving quality? The answer is teamwork. Dr. Funk spent 18 months as a visiting engineer at Mitsubishi and Yokogawa Hokushin Electric and knows firsthand how Japanese corporate culture promotes effective teamwork in production, design, and technology development. Here's a penetrating case study and analysis that presents a truly viable model for the West.
ISBN 0-915299-69-0 / 508 pages / $50.00 / Order TEAMAD-B248

Productivity Press, Inc. Dept. BK, P.O. Box 13390, Portland, OR 97213-0390
Telephone: 1-800-394-6868   Fax: 1-800-394-6286

The Unshackled Organization
Facing the Challenge of Unpredictability
Through Spontaneous Reorganization
Jeffrey Goldstein

Managers should not necessarily try to solve all the internal problems within their organizations; intervention may help in the short term, but in the long run may inhibit true problem-solving change from taking place. And change is the real goal. Through change comes real hope for improvement. Using leading-edge scientific and social theories about change, Goldstein explores how change happens within an organization and reveals that only through "self organization" can natural, lasting change occur. This book is a pragmatic guide for managers, executives, consultants, and other change agents.
ISBN 1-56327-048-X / 208 pages / $25.00 / Order UO-B248

Handbook for Personal Productivity
Henry E. Liebling

A little book with a lot of power that will help you become more successful and satisfied at work, as well as in your personal life. This pocket-sized handbook offers sections on personal productivity improvement, team achievement, quality customer service, improving your health, and how to get the most out of workshops and seminars. Special bulk discounts are available (call for more information).
ISBN 0-915299-94-1 / 128 pages / $9.00 paper / Order PP-B248

The Idea Book
Improvement Through TEI (Total Employee Involvement)
Japan Human Relations Association

At last, a book showing how to create Total Employee Involvement (TEI) and get hundreds of ideas from each employee every year to improve every aspect of your organization. Gathering improvement ideas from your entire workforce is a must for global competitiveness. *The Idea Book,* heavily illustrated, is a hands-on teaching tool for workers and supervisors to refer to again and again. Perfect for study groups, too.
ISBN 0-915299-22-4 / 232 pages / $55.00 / Order IDEA-B248

Productivity Press, Inc. Dept. BK, P.O. Box 13390, Portland, OR 97213-0390
Telephone: 1-800-394-6868   Fax: 1-800-394-6286

Individual Motivation
Removing the Blocks to Creative Involvement
Etienne Minarik

The key to gaining the competitive advantage in a saturated market is to use existing resources more efficiently and creatively. This book shows managers how to turn employees' "negative individualism" into creativity and initiative. It describes the shift in corporate culture necessary to enable front-line employees to use their knowledge about product and process to the company's greatest benefit.
ISBN 0-915299-85-2 / 263 pages / $30.00 / Order INDM-B248

Kaizen Teian 1
Developing Systems for Continuous Improvement
Through Employee Suggestions
Japan Human Relations Association (ed.)

Especially relevant for middle and upper managers, this book focuses on the role of managers as catalysts in spurring employee ideas and facilitating their implementation. It explains how to run a proposal program on a day-to-day basis and outlines the policies that support a "bottom-up" system of innovation and defines the three main objectives of *kaizen teian:* to build participation, develop individual skills, and achieve higher profits.
ISBN 0-915299-89-5 / 217 pages / $40.00 / Order KT1-B248

Kaizen Teian 2
Guiding Continuous Improvement
Through Employee Suggestions
Japan Human Relations Association (ed.)

Building on the concepts covered in *Kaizen Teian I,* this second volume examines in depth how to implement kaizen teian—a continuous improvement suggestions system. Managers will learn techniques for getting employees to think creatively about workplace improvements and how to run a successful proposal program.
ISBN 0-915299-53-4 / 221 pages / $40.00 / Order KT2-B248

Productivity Press, Inc. Dept. BK, P.O. Box 13390, Portland, OR 97213-0390
Telephone: 1-800-394-6868   Fax: 1-800-394-6286

The Service Industry Idea Book
Employee Involvement in Retail and Office Improvement
Japan Human Relations Association (ed.)

This book presents an improvement proposal system designed especially for customer service and administrative employees. Initial chapters about why suggestions are important and how to write persuasive improvement proposals are followed by two chapters of illustrated examples and case histories from various services industries and office and administrative situations.
ISBN 0-915299-65-8 / 294 pages / $50.00 / Order SIDEA-B248

TO ORDER: Write, phone, or fax Productivity Press, Dept. BK, P.O. Box 13390, Portland, OR 97213-0390, phone 1-800-394-6868, fax 1-800-394-6286. Send check or charge to your credit card (American Express, Visa, MasterCard accepted).

U.S. ORDERS: Add $5 shipping for first book, $2 each additional for UPS surface delivery. We offer attractive quantity discounts for bulk purchases of individual titles; call for more information.

INTERNATIONAL ORDERS: Write, phone, or fax for quote and indicate shipping method desired. For international callers, telephone number is 503-235-0600 and fax number is 503-235-0909. Prepayment in U.S. dollars must accompany your order (checks must be drawn on U.S. banks). When quote is returned with payment, your order will be shipped promptly by the method requested.

NOTE: Prices are in U.S. dollars and are subject to change without notice.

Productivity Press, Inc. Dept. BK, P.O. Box 13390, Portland, OR 97213-0390
Telephone: 1-800-394-6868   Fax: 1-800-394-6286